RELIGION IN THE POST-WAR WORLD

EDITED BY WILLARD L. SPERRY VOLUME II

RELIGION AND OUR DIVIDED DENOMINATIONS
By Willard L. Sperry; John LaFarge, S.J.; John Thomas McNeill; Louis Finkelstein; Archibald MacLeish.

RELIGION OF SOLDIER AND SAILOR
By Paul D. Moody; Lucien Price; John E. Johnson; William D. Cleary; Elisha Atkins.

RELIGION AND OUR RACIAL TENSIONS
By Clyde Kluckhohn; Everett R. Clinchy; Edwin R. Embree; Margaret Mead; Bradford S. Abernethy.

RELIGION AND EDUCATION
By Alexander Meiklejohn; Payson Smith; Howard Mumford Jones; Victor L. Butterfield; Theodore Ferris.

LONDON : HUMPHREY MILFORD

OXFORD UNIVERSITY PRESS

RELIGION OF
SOLDIER and SAILOR

*One of a series of volumes on Religion
in the Post-War World, edited by Dean
Willard L. Sperry*

BY

PAUL D. MOODY
LUCIEN PRICE
JOHN E. JOHNSON
WILLIAM D. CLEARY
ELISHA ATKINS

Cambridge
HARVARD UNIVERSITY PRESS
1945

239
M77
2

CONTENTS

INTRODUCTION

THIS volume in the series is an attempt to understand what war does to the soul of the man in arms. If he was a man of faith when he entered the service, can he keep his faith? If he brought little religion or none to the day of his proving, will he become a cynic or a convert?

We have perhaps ten million of our young men in uniform. They are a cross section of our democracy. What is their heritage from the First World War and the dubious years between the two World Wars? What moral and spiritual equipment do they bring to the day of their own personal proving? What is organized religion doing for these men through the chaplaincies of the Army and the Navy? How far are the chaplains succeeding in the present emergency in meeting the naked needs of the men to whom they minister? And what of the soldier's own reflections on his experience of battle? To these problems the chapters of this book address themselves.

Our contributors have been honest and realistic. There is no sentimentality here; no cheap ecclesiastical optimism; nor is there on the other hand any disillusionment. Our writers are to be identified as follows:

Paul D. Moody is now associate minister of the First

Presbyterian Church in New York City. He was for many years President of Middlebury College in Vermont. During the First World War he was G.H.Q. chaplain of the A.E.F., first as assistant and then as successor to Bishop Brent as senior chaplain.

Lucien Price is a man of letters resident in Boston, author of several volumes, and editorial writer for the *Boston Globe*. He is also a contributor to the *Atlantic Monthly*, the *Yale Review*, and numerous other publications.

Chaplain (Captain) John E. Johnson is the senior chaplain at the Great Lakes Naval Training Station just outside Chicago. Few men have had the opportunity which has been his to appraise the "raw recruit."

Chaplain (Colonel) William D. Cleary has been, until most recently, Commandant of the Chaplain School of the United States Army, which from 1942 to 1944 was stationed at Harvard. Nearly 7000 chaplains of all faiths passed through the School under his jurisdiction. He was an honored and beloved member of the Harvard community during those years, and we value this permanent record of his task. Colonel Cleary has now been transferred to the Office of the Chief of Chaplains in Washington.

Elisha Atkins is a recent graduate of Harvard, A.B. *magna cum laude*, 1942. He enlisted in the Marine Corps in July of that year, was wounded at Cape Gloucester in New Guinea, and is now in this country in the United States Marine Corps Reserve.

Harvard University
Cambridge, Massachusetts

Willard L. Sperry
Editor

Religion of
Soldier and Sailor

✦1✦

The Precedent of the First World War

THERE is an oft-repeated paradox to the effect that the only thing that history teaches us is that history teaches us nothing. Mankind, and especially the church, should remember this when within one generation we are again engaged in a second and more terrible global war. We said during the First World War that it was waged to end wars. We could not have said this if we had not held conceptions of both war and peace that were altogether too superficial. We have talked about war as though it were a cause. It is never a cause—it is always a result. And World War II, which we may well pray will be the last, developed solely because we made no headway against those evils which inevitably result in war. Mankind has worried, in this as in so much else, about the symptoms and not sufficiently about the disease.

This is why the church made the showing it did in World War I and why it is making the showing it is in the present war; and it is the reason why this second war is so much more disastrous and costly in every way than the first. That sentence is deliberately so worded that it cannot offend those who are able to find satisfaction in the record of the church in the first war, as well as those who feel otherwise.

The attempt is here made to point out some of the lessons the prior war should have taught us in the church. Perhaps the most important is the danger of divisions in the church. For the divisions in the church were horizontal as well as vertical. The division between Catholicism and Protestantism is, alas, not the only division. If the divisions within Catholicism are less evident than the divisions within Protestantism, they are nevertheless there. And they are always there among Protestants and Catholics when the emphasis falls on the differences rather than on the things held in common—on the things at the circumference, rather than on the things which are central. It is a truism that the nearer we get to the top of the hill, the nearer we get to each other. It is those about the base of the hill who are farthest apart. There are those who are Englishmen, Frenchmen, Germans, Americans, or Russians before they are sons of God. In other words, nationalism transcends religion in their minds and lives. So, of course, they go to war.

But when the great things came in sight and were felt, the differences tended to fade into insignificance. The chaplains felt this. The lovable and broad-minded Father Duffy used to say, playfully, that it was "perfectly scandalous the way Protestants and Catholics got along together."

The first time I ever met that gallant figure was when he came to see Bishop Brent to plead for more *Protestant* chaplains for his famous division. In similar vein it is recorded that a certain machine gun battalion in the 27th Division was found, on a hurried census, to be 100 per cent Catholic. Everyone was surprised until the service records of the men were studied. Then it was found, as had been suspected, that about 50 per cent were Protestants; yet they had all enrolled themselves as Catholics, they explained, "for the duration of the war," fearing that if it were known how many Protestants there were in the battalion, their beloved chaplain—a priest—might be transferred. Many of the friendships made between Protestant ministers and Roman Catholic priests in the chaplaincy continue to this day, and these men are more conscious of the things they have in common than they are of the things which separate them. And I recall the warm friendship between a priest and a rabbi—though the acquaintance began with a dreadful quarrel. Twice when I have undertaken a new task the earliest letters of good wishes have come from priests I have not seen for years. I believe we may look for the same thing after this war.

If sometimes we are distressed at the differences between the Allies, and see in them danger to the ultimate peace we all hope for, we should be equally, if not more, distressed at the differences between the great branches of the church of Christ. The powers of darkness know the dreadful force of the saying, "Divide and conquer." When any communion makes great things small and small things great, clear-sighted men lose their interest and their faith and slip away; for they feel—and who shall say wrongly—that the God they acknowledge in their hearts is not interested in the tithing of mint, anise, and cummin. We cannot make mountains out of molehills without so impairing our vision that we come ultimately to consider mountains as molehills.

We are not pleading for uniformity—which is probably an undesirable thing—but for unity, an altogether different thing, as St. Paul made clear. The Army is made up of infantry, artillery, the air and the tank corps, and endless other branches—and the service of each different—but they have a common aim and purpose, and complement and supplement each other's service. This lesson learned in the last war is being reëmphasized. The same thing is true of our beliefs. Probably some of our differences are actually needed in the Kingdom of God. We cannot all worship in exactly the same way; but that does not matter if we remember we worship the same God.

Another lesson we should have learned is that religion and churchmanship are not necessarily the same thing and certainly not coextensive. In what some have considered the best book of its kind which came out of the last war, *Thoughts on Religion at the Front*, by the late Bishop Neville S. Talbot, there is a passage we would do well to take to heart. The conclusion which war experience drives home, he says, is this:

The special strain and pressure of war cannot elicit from the majority of men, the religion which is occupied with the saving of self. The spiritual law is that we find our life by losing it, not by saving it. In a vague and unexpressed way, as they show again and again, by their cheerfulness and unconcernedness, hosts of men in this war have laid hold on this law. They have found a purpose to which to cleave, something to give themselves away for. Only it is hardly acknowledged but rather lies below the level of mental apprehension and expression. It is the function of Christianity to raise this unacknowledged trustfulness and self-giving out of dumb subconsciousness and to give to it speech and to crown it with the glory of fully human self-devotion.

What Dr. Talbot says so well may be illustrated by a story told me in a train in France by one who knew the circumstances. There was, in a certain company in an American regiment, a soldier who had not been particularly amenable to Army discipline—sometimes drunk and often in the guardhouse. His captain was exasperated and on the point of taking drastic steps. Then the company went over the top, but was driven back to its trench by enemy fire. The captain was left wounded, not fatally, in No Man's Land. This particular soldier crawled out from the comparative safety of the trench and lay down beside the captain who had disciplined him, offering his body as a screen between the wounded captain and the German machine guns. When, later reinforced, the company was able to advance again, they found the captain, who had received one more slight wound, still alive and salvageable. But they found the soldier dead beside him—his body riddled with machine gun bullets from his head to his heels. He had deliberately laid his body down as a living screen. Certain familiar texts of Scripture come back to mind. Here is one form of religion and by no means the poorest. Along the same line is the old story of a sailor who dived overboard from a vessel at sea at great risk to his own life and saved the life of a drowning man. He was approached by a pious soul and asked if when he leaped to the rescue and the possibility of his own death, he was prepared to meet his God. He replied, "I wouldn't have been any more prepared if I had let the poor devil drown."

To quote Dr. Talbot again, "There is then little conscious and articulate Christianity at the front and yet there are profoundly Christian characteristics in what men are and do and endure who have never known or do not understand or have forgotten the Christian religion." Again words of the Master come rushing back: "Not every one that saith Lord, Lord . . ." and "By their fruits ye shall know them."

A friend of mine was sobered and enlightened by an experience he had in speaking to a group of soldiers. He sought from them their ideas as to the cardinal sins. He thought they would say gambling, drinking, impurity, swearing. He was surprised when they laughed at him and answered, cowardice, selfishness, laziness, and carelessness. In other words, sins of the flesh did not shock them as much as sins of the spirit. Well, there was One who expressed more hope for the publican and the harlot than for the Scribes and Pharisees.

The chaplains who come back from this war (and many

will not come, God rest them), will have many such stories to tell. Some who cannot tell them have done better, for they have told with their lives. The instance of four chaplains on a sinking ship, taking off their life preservers and giving them to men who did not have them and kneeling in prayer—Protestant, Catholic, and Jew—as the ship went down, is the sort of thing we are talking about.

Men who have looked upon this kind of religion may be pardoned if they are not precisely enthusiastic on their return at an invitation to the chicken supper, Friday night, of the Methodist Church. Elijah found in zeal and bewilderment that there were seven thousand who had not bowed the knee to Baal. The membership of the Church Visible and the Church Invisible will always be found to differ.

It must be stated flatly that, for whatever reason, the church after the last war was not able to capitalize upon this real, if inarticulate, religion. All too often what the church offered made small appeal. There are posts of the American Legion in different parts of the country, even some accused of too much part in politics, which have taken a keener and more enlightened interest in the welfare, for example, of young boys and done more for them in practical ways than some churches.

As for a precedent in the First World War as to what the church—or more properly the churches—did, it is necessary to turn to the record of the chaplains in the last war. The present war came upon us, in the end, so suddenly that it was not anticipated as we now see it should have been. The growth of pacifism in the churches had made any preparations for the crisis difficult. If the War Department was not ready for the role it had to assume, it did, in spite of this, a remarkable piece of work which is recognized by everyone. The same thing is true of the Navy. It cannot be said that we are a militaristic people or that we wanted war, and our unpreparedness is all the evidence that is needed. In the present crisis we did enact selective service legislation practically fifteen months before the attack on Pearl Harbor, and there were still in the service, fortunately, many men like General Marshall, General MacArthur, and many of the other leaders who had had the experience of World War I. We were nowhere near so inexperienced, and progress had been made in the development both of the Regular Army and the Reserves and the National Guard. Staff work and maneuvers and training in general were so far ahead of what they had been in 1917 that there can be no comparison. In the country at large the people as a whole had learned that war was possible as they had not realized it prior to 1914. The development of the airplane and the submarine and other arms of the service had gone ahead. In the First World War a year and more went by before units could be sent to the battle front in sufficient strength to be felt, and our principal contribution in the first year of our participation was, as in the present war, far more on the industrial side. So, those whose memories are short or who are too young to remember, can form little conception of the difficulties to be overcome in the early stages of the First World War. They were mental as well as material. It was hard to believe that such an anachronism

as war was possible, and in the forefront of this incredulity
stood the churches with a viewpoint based more on idealism
than realism. The Y.M.C.A. and the Red Cross, with their
international contacts, were not taken so completely by
surprise; and their organizations lent themselves more readily to the necessary adjustments. That is why they were
often relatively better prepared than Congress or the Army
or the Navy. And far better prepared than the church,
which had no agency sufficient for the strain of united action, and which, in addition—weakened and distracted by
pacifism—was in no position to act as a unit.

Consequently, when the First World War broke upon
us, the facilities for ministering to the spiritual needs of the
men in service were utterly disorganized, if the word disorganized can be applied to the almost nonexistent. In the
Regular Army of the United States there were sixty chaplains, many of them near the age limit and some of them
survivors of those unhappy days when appointments to the
chaplaincy were a matter of political patronage. This situation happily came to an end in 1913. The association of
these men was the association of peas in a bag. Each was independent of everyone else and answerable only to his commanding officer who might, and again who might not, be
sympathetic with the idea of a chaplaincy. To some commanding officers, let us admit it, the chaplain was a barely
tolerated nuisance. He was, with the possible exception of
the Catholic chaplains, more or less orphaned from his denomination. Promotion, which means so much in the Army,
was very slow; and the pressure to consider himself an offi-

cer rather than a clergyman was constant and almost atmospheric. He became of necessity more or less regimentally minded, with small inducement to feel responsibility outside his own regiment or post, and the atmosphere in most posts was generally rather somnolent, for war seemed very remote. Such things as chaplains' schools were undreamed of in those days. Appointments were made by an amiable lady who served as clerk in the office of the Adjutant General, and sometimes assignments were most unwisely made. Many regiments predominantly Catholic had Protestant chaplains, and vice versa, and small provision was made to correct this situation. Moreover, contact with the type of enlisted man found in the Army in peacetime did not always prepare the chaplain for the type of man who enlisted in the face of danger and from the highest motives.

In the National Guard things were hardly, if any, better. Many of the Militia regiments had as chaplains clergymen who in civilian life occupied fairly important pulpits, but of course in most cases these clergymen, busy with their normal parishes, could hardly spare even the two weeks of the summer muster, and apart from this they were quite untrained. As a general thing, however, it is not too unfair to say that the demands of parish life had had a tendency to keep them a little more alive. At any rate, it was found in France that the National Guard chaplains were able to adjust themselves better to the changed and enlarged conditions brought about by the war than some of the regulars whom age and long service in the quiet of peacetime posts had unfitted for increased responsibilities.

With the outbreak of hostilities and the immediate formation of what was then called the National Army, to the Divisions of which the draftees were largely sent, the need for more chaplains was immediately evident and many were commissioned as Reserve chaplains for the duration. Later, for the benefit of these, a school was started. The value of this school as then conducted has been questioned, since it was almost entirely manned by chaplains whose experience was largely limited to tours of duty in the Philippines or long experience in the somnolent atmosphere of peacetime posts. It was the experience of many of the men who passed through the various sessions of the school that the curriculum, which lasted for only six weeks, was too much taken up with the study of matters that were of relatively little value in France. Certainly many who came to us in France were woefully unprepared for what they faced.

War had been going on for a full year before any attempt was made to organize the work of the chaplains in France. It was claimed by some that inertia on the part of the chaplains who should have taken the lead, and a certain perhaps unconscious mutual denominational jealousy, were instrumental in holding back the men who should have taken the initiative. This is hard to say. Whatever the reason may have been, nothing was done until, in April 1918, the Commander in Chief of the A.E.F., General Pershing, asked Bishop Brent to convene a board to make recommendations looking to greater usefulness on the part of the chaplains and a closer coördination of their efforts with the efforts of the various welfare agencies. These agencies were in many cases better equipped to do and, in some instances, were doing what the chaplains would normally be supposed to do. The Red Cross had, for example, a number of special or Red Cross chaplains, and these were doing excellent work in the hospitals. A great many ministers who had volunteered to go over with the Y.M.C.A. were also serving as volunteer chaplains where Army chaplains were unavailable. The Knights of Columbus had brought over some priests who had been attached as volunteer workers in those regiments which had a large number of Catholics, yet Protestant chaplains. All these various agencies, General Pershing felt, could be more effective with some coördination and oversight. This would prevent, it was hoped, overlapping and duplication of effort, and avoid conflict and friction. How far it succeeded is not for me to say.

This board, which consisted of Bishop Brent as chairman, Chaplain Francis B. Dougherty, and the writer, met at Headquarters, A.E.F., early in April 1918 and made their recommendations. There was a certain degree of distribution of representation on this board. Bishop Brent was at this time serving as liaison officer between the C. in C. and the Y.M.C.A., and was, as everyone knows, an Episcopalian who had covered himself with distinction by his service as Missionary Bishop of the Philippines, where he had formed a large acquaintance with the Army. Chaplain Dougherty was a regular who had entered the service at the time of the

Spanish American War and was the representative of the Roman Catholic Church and the Regular Army. The writer, a Congregationalist, was a National Guard chaplain whose commission was a year and a half old, but he alone of the three had had front-line experience, however brief, in the First World War.

The report, or findings, of this board, with recommendations, was forwarded, and the members returned to their posts. Three weeks later a special order was issued creating the board as a permanent board and instructing and empowering it to carry out as far as possible the recommendations which it had made. The order was dated the 26th of April, 1918, and the board functioned from that date, known as the General Headquarters Chaplains Office, with Bishop Brent as chairman, a position he held till the virtual discharge of the Board and the transfer of administration to the Army of Occupation a year later. Then the Senior Chaplain of the Army of Occupation, with Headquarters at Coblenz, took over what remained to be done. Bishop Brent, contrary to what is usually thought, did not become a chaplain till after the war, because Army regulations interfered. He was commissioned as a major in the Adjutant General's office and *assigned* to the Board of Chaplains in this capacity.

As far as we know, this was the first time in the history of the American Army that any attempt was made to organize the work of the chaplains. The authority of this Board was confined entirely to the A.E.F., and had nothing whatever to do with the chaplains in this country, who remained for the most part as unorganized at the end as they were at the beginning of the war. It was after the war that the War Department—influenced by the experience in France—adopted some of the recommendations of the Board, and a chief of chaplains was appointed.

In the meantime, the Navy, which by its very nature is differently organized, appointed a ranking chaplain as chief of chaplains, and this appointment accounts for what a former Army chaplain like myself is so loath to admit, a better organization of the Navy chaplains in the last war.

The situation in this country remained anomalous. It was as disorganized as it was possible for it to be. Let us hasten to admit it was also somewhat disorganized in the A.E.F., despite the appointment of a board. But it was probably on the whole better in France than here. Meanwhile the War-Time Commission of the Churches was formed in this country. This was a relatively small group, but it contained some of the most honored names among Protestant clergymen, and even one or two laymen. It was headed by Bishop Lawrence of Massachusetts, and Bishop McDowell of the Methodist Church was its constant representative in Washington. It was the wish of this board that some arrangement similar to that existing in the A.E.F. should be set up here, and the matter was going forward when the Armistice was signed and all further action brought to a standstill. This War-Time Commission had no official standing with the War Department, but because of its personnel it had considerable weight. In the light of subsequent developments it is to be regretted that circumstances did not permit it to go further in its plans and recommendations. Its work ended too soon.

On the signing of the Armistice, of course, the first thought of everyone was to get back home and out of uniform. The word "disintegration" is not too strong. We had all been held by a common purpose up to that hour. Now the individualistic tendencies of men came out and each man thought of his home and his work. The tendencies up to the 11th hour of the 11th day of the 11th month had been centripetal. Now, in one brief day, they became centrifugal. The cement of one great common purpose was gone. The churches which had gladly sent their ministers were clamoring loudly for their return; the chaplains no less than the rank and file were anxious to have it over with, and it was nearly impossible to interest anyone in the chaplaincy as a life work. So the War-Time Commission disbanded, and its work, dwindling from a broad stream to a trickle, was undertaken by a committee of the Federal Council of Churches of Christ in America. In certain quarters this Council was suspect on the grounds of pacifism and in others on the ground of socialism, both probably unfairly. To its credit, the Army in its plans for reorganization did take an interest in the chaplaincy. But since it had lost all the Reserve chaplains and retained only the regular chaplains, the plans looked backward rather than forward. I doubt if it is unfair to say that some of those who remained in the service would have welcomed a return to the status quo ante. But those in control, seeing what benefits could be gained from a closer organization of the chaplains, insisted that the benefits of the lessons learned should not be thrown away; accordingly, a chaplains' corps was formed and a Chief of Chaplains was appointed with the rank of colonel. From that time on dates much of the improvement in the chaplaincy, so that today no chaplain goes into service as utterly unprepared as the chaplains of 1917. Then the only provision in the quartermaster's office for him was a chaplain's flag. If he had any of the other equipment he needed, it was because he had influence in some quarters. He had no communion sets, no car, no typewriter. If he had them, he was fortunate if they were not commandeered. My own personal typewriter went up to regimental headquarters for a long period, though with my consent. Now there are chapels where possible, and the table of organization provides nearly everything the chaplain can want; in most cases the denomination steps in and furnishes what the Army does not, vestments and the like. Then the denominations were too often quite blind to the need of their ministers in the service.

The church as a whole has lost an opportunity, for it should work hand in glove with the War Department, and not merely serve, as the General Commission of Army and Navy Chaplains does, as a sort of recruiting agency with little or no authority and occupied for the most part with gathering the denominational endorsements of candidates.

This is the more true because the War Department as a result of its experience in 1917-18 has changed the whole arrangement. The U.S.O. has taken the place of the various welfare agencies, and is under closer Army control. At the same time the position of the chaplain has been clarified and he is freer from some of the encroachments on his time which he knew then. He no longer serves as Canteen Officer, Postmaster, and Athletic Officer, or is asked to do the many things which interfered with his more spiritual duties. And, while he is answerable to his commanding officer, he has the satisfaction of being under the sympathetic supervision of more experienced men in the chaplaincy to whom he may look for guidance and direction, and, in some cases, protection in the discharge of the duties which are peculiarly his.

In brief, whatever lessons were not learned in the First World War, these, of interest to the church, certainly were. First, that the chaplains can do a notable and highly useful work and contribute greatly to morale if given a chance, as they were when they received sympathetic and intelligent oversight and direction and were relieved of all the multitudinous nonecclesiastical duties too often wished upon them in the past by officers who did not always understand too clearly the proper function of a chaplain. To this end they must be provided with those things necessary to make them more effective. The church's greatest service could be rendered in the selection of the right men for this work and in support for them when selected.

Secondly: welfare agencies like the Y.M.C.A., the Red Cross, the Knights of Columbus, the Salvation Army, and the Jewish Welfare board, however excellent and useful and well meaning, cannot profitably be allowed to operate as semi-independent institutions, as *imperia in imperio*,

apart from the closest Army supervision. Whatever criti-
cisms arose, just or unjust, were in a measure due to the too-
great degree of independence they had in the last war. That
is why in the present war morale has become a duty of and
a part of the office of the Adjutant General and why there
is today the U.S.O. The government, whether through the
Army or the Navy, has the final responsibility for the morale and the morals—two things even closer than the spell-
ing—of the soldiers and the sailors. It cannot delegate this.
Therefore the chaplain, appointed by the government,
must have the heaviest responsibility both to the Army or
the Navy and to the church. His work can be supplemented
and assisted by the outside agencies, and the better a chaplain is the more he will welcome such assistance and avail
himself of it. But his work cannot be supplanted by these;
the church and the Army and the Navy have discovered
this as the result of the experience of World War I.

The chaplain has an opportunity such as few have in civilian life, since he is in daily intimate touch with young
men far from home and often lonely, missing all that is familiar, in constant danger of death and faced with new and
diverse temptations and trials, with their minds constantly
turned toward the idea of duty and a task outside their
usual strength, and with sacrifice ever before their eyes. In
their better moments they are conscious of a great and often
dimly felt need. To such men the chaplain can make this
need clearer and its expression more articulate. To such
men the chaplain can point the way, bring inspiration, comfort, and courage.

⁺2⁺

Between Two Wars

In April 1919 the Yankee Division just home from France paraded in Boston. We were told they did not like it. ("What do these civilians think we are? A damn circus? The hell with them!") Hour after hour that raw, blustery day, these young soldiers, a river of youth, flowed along Tremont Street. Their faces were the study. Ruddied by exposure to weather, they were, without having been coarsened, subtly hardened. And how not? The look was unmistakable. So here marched, one knew it then, the history of these United States in the next two decades. What would this crop of youth do to those decades; and what would those decades do to them?

My next landmark occurs at Amherst College, the following spring, 1920. The professors there were saying privately, "We don't understand these boys. They are out of hand. We can't appeal to them in the pre-war terms. 'Oh, don't bother us,' they say. 'Leave us alone. And for God's sake, don't talk to us about *ideals!* We never want to hear of them again.'" Yes, but were these the young men who had been in the war, or the incoming crop who had not been? "Both!"

By 1922 a third portent was clear. The word "sin" was becoming obsolete. Now sin had been a truncheon of the morals police, to be wielded mainly by the clergy. It was, and is, still wielded to some extent by the clergy, but the young and intrepid spirits among both sexes were no longer intimidated by that truncheon. What had happened to sin? The Darwinian theory had reversed the concept of man's fall from grace in a golden age; the Marxian critique of capitalism had challenged the bourgeois ethics by which property was protected; the Freudian psychology had undercut many of the moral codes sanctioned by custom; the First World War had demolished the pretensions of the elder generation that they knew best what was good for the young—demolished, too, the very notion that the elder generation had the civilized world under any control at all —and, together with all these, had come (1) the advancing economic independence of women; (2) the internal combustion engine which had broken down whatever system of chaperonage survived; and (3) contraception.

Most of these were not causes but effects. They were effects of a single main cause—the impact of novel scientific techniques on what had seemed to be a stable society. The technological conditions of human life had changed faster between 1800 and 1919 than in the preceding 2000 years— one might perhaps say 3000 years. In science, in economics, in religion, in ethics, in the fine arts, there was hardly a concept which had not been brusquely jostled, if indeed it had not been shattered. In 1880 the Newtonian physics were considered to be as sound and fixed as the Everlasting Seat; by 1900, though still a convenient way of looking at things, they were seen to be only a half-truth, if that. As for the Everlasting Seat, it had long been a question whether there was one.

Now this sort of news travels fast. People, and quite simple people, can feel the tremor of such social earthquakes under their sole leather without needing in the least to be able to consult a seismograph; and such tremors underrun even the most august, the seemingly most impregnable institutions, which may appear to go on much as usual and as they did at any time these hundreds of years, when all the while, underneath, nothing is as usual.

II

At this point let us have an understanding. In the discussion which follows I am well aware that precision is impossible—indeed, that the substance here discussed is so immeasurable that precise definition, even if possible, would be tantamount to self-invalidation. It merely happens that this subject was the one which most occupied me in the two decades between 1919 and 1939. Like so many of my fellow countrymen, I too was seeking. The house of certitude, in everything from traditional religion to Newtonian physics, had been burnt down over my head and, like them, I was looking for some shelter that could at least keep out the weather. But as such a search goes on, one meets other seekers, we exchange experience, gradually gain some notion of how the search is progressing, and in what directions, and what, if any, pay streaks these prospectors for a celestial city, or a great society, or a good life, have struck. It is as if you had backed me up against the brick wall of Old South Meeting House in Newspaper Row on Washington Street at the noon hour and said, "Come, now. How does it look to you?" and I had replied, "Don't take my word for it; but, since you ask, this is how it looks to me." My testimony is given for whatsoever it may be worth. It may be worthless. But having watched every area of this subject accessible to me during these two decades, from newspaper print and common conversation to wide travel, sociological treatise, and historical scholarship, deponent testifieth and saith. . . . Let the reader judge, if he can.

III

The religious life of a people or of a period may be described as a barge and a towboat. The towboat is much less impressive than the barge. The barge moves grandly, perhaps even serenely and smoothly; the towboat puffs, whistles, tugs, strains, sends up volumes of black smoke, and churns quick-water astern. Aboard the barge are multitudes of estimable folk, many of them the salt of the earth, and generally far more agreeable fellow passengers than the crew of the towboat. Aboard the barge, a life of the spirit is lived mostly within the existing institutions of organized religion. Furthermore, the barge is freighted with precious heirlooms, irreplaceable works of art, beautiful furniture, and choice books. But the barge has no self-propulsion—no engines, no boilers, no fuel, no twin screws—and she answers her helm only when the towline hitched to the bits in the stern of the towboat is taut. The towboat by herself could weather quite a gale; but if the towline parted, the barge would be in a bad way.

The towboat crew (she carries no passengers) is polyglot. They are the people of actively religious spirit, bizarre as may be some of the human disguises under which it is manifested. (The sacred spring seldom bubbles up in the marble basin built for it—as like as not you may find it in the barnyard.) These disguises may be as various as that of communist labor leader or virtuoso violinist, and not omitting those obscure and devoted parsons and priests of all sects, good shepherds of their flocks, always the true strength of an organized religion.

But growth means out-growth. As a culture matures, its people of higher intelligence tend to outgrow their traditional theology. Its concepts are seen to have been oversimplified, or are too simple-minded; its ethics may prove indefensible; and, viewed as a philosophy, it is found not to include the whole of life (as Christianity is, for us, deficient both in the element of laughter and in its conception of beauty), or it may be discovered to be insufficiently workable in social conditions which are changing under the impact of novel scientific technology. All this has, within historical times, happened more than once, and it is happening in our time.

IV

External events in the United States between wars are too well remembered to need recapitulation in detail. Generalized, they are somewhat as follows:

1919 to 1929—the Jazz Decade. A generation of youth whose idealism, inherited from the nineteenth century, had been exploited in the World War of 1914-1918 and then shamelessly betrayed, went for the most part spiritually bankrupt. (This exploitation and betrayal was through no fault of Woodrow Wilson, who was himself a victim.)

Their petition into bankruptcy was involuntary. Let me cite another landmark. A retentive memory photographs by flashlight the vivid moment when some major social phenomenon first strikes one's observation. Early in 1919 when our troops had begun to return from France, a village woman who knew her own town and its history well remarked, "I remember when the boys came home from the Civil War. They were all heroes to everybody. But not much seems to be thought of our boys who are coming home now. You wouldn't think we owed them a thing. And they feel it!" She had early worded what was later to become a general observation. President Hoover in due season had the bonus army bombed out of Washington by tear gas. But even in 1919 there were some who thought they understood what had happened. If asked, they would have said that these youth, having been cynically used in a capitalistic dogfight, had been as cynically discarded. Supposing that to have been true, too few understood the first half of the process, but plenty of them could feel the second. It did not conduce to religious feeling.

Meanwhile had come Prohibition. To Jazz Decade, then, add "hooch." This law threw the liquor trade with its huge profits and consequent power, quite unexpectedly, into the hands of the criminal class. The ensuing demoralization seeped in all directions like an oilstain in a tablecloth; the young broke the law in bravado; normally law-abiding citizens broke it out of resentment; and the breaking of it broke multitudes of its breakers before it was repealed.

Money in the Jazz Decade was flush. Complexities aside, the economics of the United States between 1919 and 1929, as nearly as a layman could understand them, appeared to be somewhat as follows: (1) Buy off working-class revolt with high wages, Ford cars, silk shirts, and radios, the while your press keeps up a drumfire against "Bolshevism" and something more grim than threat at any signs of active revolt; (2) lend money by the millions to Europe, Germany especially, and to South America; keep on passing around this financial paper, with promises to pay at some future date, until October 1929, when it is suddenly discovered that next to nobody can pay anything. (Tableau. Red fire.)

One is tempted to term the decade which followed, 1929 to 1939, "The Hangover." It was that, but fortunately it was also something better. Youth rallied. And not only did youth rally, but so did most of their elders. It is of course true that bankers, brokers, and deflated stockholders after the crash walked out of tenth-story windows in such numbers that newspapers had to pepper these suicides through their inside pages instead of printing them on the front page in box-scores, as they did the Monday morning toll of motor fatalities; but it is also true that sensible and stout-hearted people, including not a few who had lost heavily in the crash, would tell you that their pioneering grandparents had not been afraid of hardscrabble, that they proposed to be as plucky as their grandparents, and further that, in their opinion, our financial hardhack after October 1929 was a far safer and more wholesome condition for our people as a whole than had been the flush finance prior to that date.

No, it was not all as admirable or as amiable as that. By 1933, the propertied classes were squawking ("squawk" is the verb) at being taxed to help support those whose labor could not be gainfully employed under the profit system of private ownership, now euphemistically (and falsely) known as "free enterprise"; and this, too, as the 1930's went on, including the unemployment of young men by the millions whose creative talents could not then be utilized to the profit of private ownership, but have been utilized since 1941 by the millions for the destruction of life and property by means of equipment costing billions of dollars.

But even so, the 1930's were sweeter years than the 1920's. Those flush years, 1919 to 1929, had been angry years. People, even people who had been poor and then found themselves with more money than they had ever expected to have in their lives, were discontented. Having margins of ease, perhaps of leisure, which nothing in their past training had taught them how to use, they were bored, disappointed, and finally bitter, like children who have come to the party only to find that it was not as much fun as they had expected it to be. In the very public prints, dailies, weeklies, monthly magazines, and books, the snapping and snarling at one another was disconcerting. Why were so many persons so angry? Times had never looked so flush; none but a few watchers of the skies were prey to forebodings of another war; the world might well prove to be America's oyster and we were eating at first table. What ailed these people?

Their ailment was that they lacked something to live for that was more important than themselves, their families, their property, or their occupations—they lacked, in one word, religion. Now you may have your religion in what form you like so it be also *sub specie aeternitatis:* that is, to live and labor for some higher than personal end, and to some greater love, "greater than wife, or child, or native land."

V

Then began the great rally of the 1930's. Primarily it was a rally of youth, but it was immensely reinforced by a rally which occurred also among their elders and especially among certain professions; principally that of education.

This had, in fact, begun much earlier. The earliest intimation of its being a major sociological event in the United States reached me in the autumn of 1926. The form it took was a sudden, if belated, realization that religion as a subject of general interest, even if not of ardent enthusi-

asm, had been supplanted by education. It was as though
the American people, secretly scandalized by the war-fever
of their clergy in 1917-18, had brought their children to
the schoolmaster and said, "The church did not save us
from the mistakes (not to use a harsher word) of the war
and afterward. Take these children, especially the boys, and
see what you can do for them. We are willing to give you
a try, for we can see that mere 'goodness,' like patriotism, is
not enough. There must be brains."

For this trend to become unmistakably evident took
about half a dozen years more. By that time it was clear that
our people had turned for their spiritual impetus from the
church to the college, from the parson to the professor. Occasionally, as in the Catholic colleges, some of them excellent ones, the clergy were the professoriates, but with the
Protestants, who constitute by far the majority of our population, this trek was externally secular.

But secular in externals only. At heart, it was spiritual
hunger which drove these herds of young deer to the scho-
lastic salt licks. And they did not fare so badly. Those who
reached in good secondary or high schools the beginnings
of the liberal arts curriculum, and more, those who were
able to go on through the liberal arts colleges and further
into professional studies and higher education, did in some
measure partake of the spiritual heritage of the western
world and the religious experience of the human race in
forms as various as scientific investigation, humane learning,
and the creative arts.

Such was the inner reality of that great trek. Its outward

manifestations were, while less real, far more spectacular. Money rained into the laps of our universities, colleges, technical schools, secondary schools, not omitting our public schools and state universities, like the shower of gold from Zeus into the lap of Danaë, until some of the more judicious friends of higher education in America began to wonder whether its virtue might be as severely compromised by this golden shower as was that of Danaë herself by Father Zeus. The shower went right on through the worst years of the financial depression, 1929 to 1933 ("If you have fortunes, prepare to shed them now"). Some, too many, of these educational beneficiaries splurged with the money. Their idea was to "build plant." Dubious, even naïve, as that course may have then seemed and been, it was perhaps accidentally fortunate, since "plant" was built when it could be; for now it may be many a decade before money will be plentiful enough for educational foundations to build plant on such a scale again. Other institutions—and theirs is the honor—built only so much plant as was necessary to provide walls, floors, and roofs to house the most excellent teaching they could obtain.

The spiritual insemination from this union of learning and life was wide and deep. For the first time in history a great nation had undertaken to educate, not alone an élite, but the whole mass of its people. As yet we had not brought the majority of them much above the literacy level at the ages of sixteen or eighteen; but we were on our way, for this country has never taken to the idea of education for an élite, though meanwhile, as always, the progress of all thought being necessarily from the individual to the mass, from the few to the many, the influence which emanated from the educated class was, as has been said, deep and wide.

VI

Between wars, meanwhile, another rhythm was generated. This one is very powerful, probably in the long wave length, more powerful even than humane learning, since it is creative instead of acquisitive, and it was evidenced at least six or seven years earlier than the other. Hardly had the troops of World War I disbanded when this became startlingly noticeable, as early as 1919 and 1920. Again, like the other between-war social phenomena, it began quietly, as great oaks from little acorns grow. One heard (now here, now there) that the heir presumptive to this factory or that bank was not interested in succeeding to his father's swivel chair. Then what, pray, *was* he going to do? Study painting, become a musician, a writer, a sculptor, a landscape architect—even an actor, God wot!—and not some of the well-to-do only, but impecunious youths and maidens also, who, having nothing to lose by the venture of faith in a creative career, might have a world to gain.

Bear in mind that our young men had not had such a physical and mental stirabout since the Civil War. Two millions of them had had a free, if involuntary, trip to Europe; and four millions of them had been haled out of their homes and herded into army camps. For the first half-dozen years between wars, 1919 to 1925, this trend of

youth toward the creative arts was not to be taken too seriously, though it would bear watching. But as the 1920's
drew to their close, economic tailspin though there was,
this trek of promising and creatively talented youth to the
arts had become a fact to reckon with—not in the weight
of its numbers but in the weight of its potentialities. It
meant that the fine arts in America were being cleared of
the black eye they had had from the Puritan of the seven-
teenth and eighteenth centuries, and, in the nineteenth,
from its hangover and from the Philistinism of material
wealth and that tyranny of the life of action over the life
of thought which had been concomitant with our conquest
of this continental wilderness. It was now the Puritan who
had the black eye, and, by 1929, the banker. For the first
time in the United States the artist, using that term in its
broadest sense, began to be treated by the public, using that
term too in its broadest sense, with the respect that had long
been accorded him in Europe.

The possessive instincts divide mankind; the creative impulses unite mankind. Aesthetic feeling, shared emotions in
the presence of beauty, are great harmonizers of "the four-
and-seventy jarring Sects." Beauty is a more inclusive term
than religion. For brotherhood, worship, and holiness are
but three of the infinite forms of beauty. And even when
we do not agree about the forms of beauty, we agree in our
love of beauty as a vital condition of existence. Like love, in
some form it is in everybody; and, again like love, without
it we die. Its unifying force acts secretly—has acted before
we know it. The union of the white and black races in

America—yes, the mixing of them—has already begun. It has begun in the fine arts. The Negro artists are on our concert platforms; their actors are on our stage; their dancers in our theaters; their folk music has penetrated our popular balladry, and spread from college choirs to symphonic scores. At the performances of their artists white and colored sit elbow-to-elbow; the question is not pigmentation of skin; the question is, is the performance moving? The color line has thus dissolved first in the region of man's highest attributes—his creative artistry—where no issue of exclusive or material possession is involved, as it is involved with those two fiercely possessive tracts, property and sex. Sex and property are immemorially the final bastions of conservative instinct: religion yields long before they do, and in truth it was by way of religious songs which the Negroes turned into folk songs of their own that this racial mixture in aesthetics first began.

VII

The eight years from 1931 to 1939 in the United States were an epoch at once of hope and of apprehension. Apprehension, from the date of the Japanese attack on Shanghai, February 1932, lest the steamship of mechanized society be no longer answering her helm; hope, since our own people were regaining confidence in themselves. We had been through a world war and an economic collapse, through an era of disenchantment, bitterness, and negation; we had rallied, were learning how to work together for social reorganization which should gradually shift our gears from excessive individualism to a moderate collectivization. Our labor movement was revitalized. Certain congressional investigations, if they did nothing else, at least enabled the vast newspaper-reading public to identify some of its internal enemies. We were learning disagreeable facts about ourselves, and facing them. Mr. John Steinbeck's *Grapes of Wrath* was a national event. Two opposite discoveries were proceeding in this same epoch: the accelerated discovery of ghastly wastage in our natural resources and in our human potentialities, wastage as various as in oil deposits, dust bowls, and share-croppers; and the discovery of our immense reserves of energy, which have, since Pearl Harbor, been resoundingly demonstrated all the way from the fighting fronts to the assembly lines. This growing realization by the people of their own strength was frightening in certain quarters, and it produced among us, by the same process as in the Axis nations, certain Fascist counterparts. For Fascism is capitalism gone nudist. The hope of these parafascist gentry was toward a western capitalist coalition against Soviet Russia, and if you want a key to the tortuous diplomatic maneuvering in the last half-dozen years before the Second World War, this is it.

Like a powerful drama, that decade from 1929 to 1939 began with a bang and ended with a bang. It began with financial collapse; it ended in World War II. Most of the years between were uneasy and anxious, and yet all the while this nation was the richest on earth, and the richest nation that had ever lived on earth. The form our riches had taken was peculiar. It was neither mineral nor vegetable, though we were rich in both. Neither was it mechanical, though there, too, we were richer than anybody else. Our unique and peculiar riches were in a form so common that most of us thought no more of it than of the air we breathed. Our riches were human, and of this worth and value, the most highly concentrated deposit, the finest mintage in the noblest metal, were our young men.

Eleven millions of them—they may soon be twelve—are in the armed forces. Expendable or not, we can ill afford to spend them. They are the ultimate savings bank account of our existence as a people, of our future as a nation, of our earthly immortality as a spiritually creative force. For three centuries on a virgin continent these savings had been accumulating. The physical conditions had been unprecedentedly advantageous: climate, temperate and bracing; forests and fields, rivers and ranges, shores and seas, all inviting to adventure and to a schooling in resourcefulness and self-reliance. In the main, too, it was that struggle of man against natural obstacles which can be one of his most ennobling disciplines. Add to this, that the racial stocks embarked on this North American adventure were self-selected, at least until the mid-nineteenth century, from the pick of Europe. The interdependence of pioneering conditions made us equalitarian in spirit. You do not high-hat the neighbor whose ax you may need to borrow, and whose rifle may save your sconce from the scalping-knife. Then, as these vital dangers ceased, we were left with the unconscious assumption that "Nobody will harm me, if I don't harm him." This bred a gracious, kindly type of youth, which, while not unique in history, existed on these shores in far greater numbers than it had ever existed before anywhere. It is on the perpetuation of this spirit that the continuance of our free institutions must depend, since laws, customs, and constitutions are founded only secondarily on how people think, but primarily on how they feel. And now eleven million young men, whose creative talents could not in anything like their totality be gainfully employed under the profit system of private ownership between 1929 and 1933, and after, have been trained to use the machines of scientific technology for the destruction of life and property. "Theirs not to reason why": they were conscripted. You tell me the war was forced on us. I reply, the verdict of the future will be that these wars were fought to decide which group of national units was to control the new techniques of production, transport, and communication. Naturally, we feel that this had better be done by us. But if in the winning we shall have lost in the slaughter of our young men that which constitutes whatsoever superiority we may possess, what have we won?

VIII

Here let us renew our understanding as of the outset. On the morning after Armistice Day, 1918, someone remarked that the question before the house was, "Where do we go from here?" It still is. As the next two decades unrolled, that question became more and more glaring. It glared out of every quarter from economics and politics to problems of conduct, of aesthetics, and the relation of

scientific innovation to human control ("Look you, how
pale he glares!"), but in no form and cause conjoined did
it glare more disconcertingly than in that of religion. Now
whatsoever value such an inquiry as this may have is that
the writer try to speak such truth as may be in him, and
that is what I do, always mindful that what I say may have
no validity for anybody but myself. Here, then, I expect
that most of you will bid me a sad farewell, though more,
I hope, in sorrow than in anger.

Our young men are being killed, maimed, or mentally
scarred. They have been subjected to military training
which is the reverse of our democratic system. War is no
school for humane thought. If anyone question this, let him
reread his Thucydides. Our American system of education
is riddled from top to bottom, and whether it can ever
be reconstituted for the effective dissemination of humane
learning remains to be seen. That block of our population
which is being exposed to these experiences of physical
and mental violence, namely the young men, is that part
of our people which is creatively the most vital. Presumably
those who survive will some day come home; there will be
ghastly gaps in their ranks, as there were in those of that
parade on Tremont Street in April 1919, only next time
they will be wider and deeper; and no doubt the faces, too,
besides being ruddied by exposure to the weather will,
for faces so young, look curiously hardened. They will
have confronted such horrors as reduce the threat of hell
in some future existence to a joke. Did institutionalized

Christianity take a bad beating after the previous war? It will take a worse one after this war, if indeed this war prove to have had anything which, within this present century, can be termed an end.

Then why speak of the two mid-war decades at all? Are they not already as dead as Pharaoh—save in such potentialities as they may have had for our future? It is precisely of those potentialities that I speak. They were, I believe, what was then initiated among us that tended toward education and religion. Those two for us, I believe, were on their way to be very close together. Were you to ask me what the people of these United States, underneath the infinite complex of all their manifold activities, were at heart doing in those twenty years between wars, I would be strongly tempted to say that, whether aware of it or not, they were seeking a religion of their own.

Why seeking? Had we not one already? Were not our chances of finding a better very slight? It was not a question of better or worse: it had become a question of validity. For as those two decades went on, the incongruity, the un-congeniality to the west and the impracticability of those religions which derive from oriental origins, became, I think, glaringly evident. Organized religions may have kept many, perhaps most, of the sectaries aboard the barge at the end of the towline. But the crew aboard the towboat were casting off that line and heading for new seas.

New seas? New seas are immemorially old ones. If there is a shore to one of these ancient seas of the human spirit which can provision us in the age to come, I know of no other rich enough, or deep enough in the soil of wisdom and creative fertility but that of ancient Hellas. As our world turns, and turns perforce from the oversimplified and impossibly perfectionist ideals of Christianity to the manifold creative one of a complex society, we are impelled toward Hellas for the simple reason that there is no place else to go.

The will to create is in all men and all women. Its forms are as various as the sexual creation of lovely and laughing children at one end of the human scale and spine, to the loftiest creations by men of genius at the other end of the human spine and the human scale. What balm to their hurt minds can we offer our young men when they come home? Bread for their bodies? If that be not offered, they will take it anyhow, as they should. Bread of the spirit then? And where shall that be found? Where but in the employment from top to bottom of the human scale, where but in the unfoldment and training of whatsoever creative capacity there be in all our people—even unto the least of these? There shall be found bread of the spirit.

This is a large order, is it? Two world wars and one economic collapse within a single life-span is a large order, too. The impact of unprecedented scientific techniques upon a once stable society is a large order. We live in an epoch of large orders, and unless we learn to think of our future in terms of large orders we are not likely to have one. A society animated by reverence for beauty in all of its infinite forms is a large order. But it would be sound; for the noblest creative activity has to do with beauty. And whether acknowledged or not, whether realized or not, in whatsoever form it may assume from children of the body to children of the spirit, from nature to human nature, beauty is the religion of all souls.

·3·

The Faith and Practice of the Raw Recruit

ANYONE who attempts to write about "The Faith and Practice of the Raw Recruit" might easily become as involved as the woman who, at the first of the year, wrote:

Dear Sir:

I hate to disturb you at such a funny time of the year but I would like to find something out.

Did a group of boys come from Omaha Nebraska on Dec 30 at nite and get there on the morning of Dec. 31. If so will you have some one ask which one remember the girl in the Red Coat and with that black hat over to one side. The one standing by the girl with the green coat and wine sweater. The one that got off at Panama, Iowa. The one they were talking to in the opposite car in the train.

I can describe him too. He has black, sorta wavy, hair, and he had a blueish plade shirt on. That's all I could see.

If you find the one tell him to write to this address ammediately. . . .

It's a matter of *life*. . . .

(Signed) . . . .

P.S. I'm praying so you find him for her.
P.S. If you find him and he doesn't know what to write will you just send his address and she will answer. It is very important.

II

In plaid shirts and coats of many colors, in zoot suits, overalls, creased or baggy pants, in Panama hats, toboggan caps, felt hats, and with no hats at all, they come in groups of a few, fifty, or a hundred and fifty. At all times of the day and night they disembark from trains at Downey Station, or at Great Lakes, enter Camp Barry at Gate 2, and proceed along the "Street of Broken Dreams" where they are frequently greeted by the oldtimers (men who have been in uniform a week or a day) who call out from a passing truck or from across the street, "You'll be s-o-r-r-y!"

Their immediate destination is Building N in the Receiving Unit. If they arrive late at night and are hungry, they are given something to eat, issued bedding and assigned places to sleep in Building X. If they arrive on Saturday afternoon, they may find themselves in Church on Sunday morning before they are in uniform.

On Monday morning and on other mornings in the week the "human assembly line" starts in front of a battery of typewriters; it passes through dental offices; it pauses on a deck (floor) marked off in sections four feet by two, where every stitch of clothing is removed and prepared for express-shipment home (collect). The line moves on through shower baths and up the ladder (stairway) to hospital corpsmen and medical officers, including psychiatrists.

III

The men who entered Building N in coats of many colors emerge in coats of one color, and are marched off by companies. One of the amazing things about Recruit Training is the company spirit that comes into being almost immediately after a company of men is formed. A hundred and twenty men from many states, North and South, East and West, from cities, towns, villages, and countrysides, are brought together. Most of these men have never seen each other before. Yet, it seems that in a matter of hours they are welded into a single unit in which each merges his interest and efforts for the good of the company. There are, of course, differences of opinion, differences in religion, differences in politics. But so strong is the company spirit that sometimes men who should turn in at sick bay for medical treatment avoid doing so as long as possible, in order to remain with their company.

They are very generous, too, and respond quickly to emergencies affecting their shipmates. If serious illness or death in the immediate family of a man requires his presence at home, the slightest intimation that there is need for funds brings forth a willingness and eagerness to contribute money to meet the need. In this regard it is necessary that careful steps be taken to protect the men against their generous impulses. The Navy Relief Society and the

American Red Cross are prepared to assist in all such emergencies.

Men have come to Great Lakes with degrees from leading universities. There was an apprentice seaman with degrees from Princeton University and from Union Theological Seminary. Illiterates, too, have come—white and colored. During the first few months of 1944 there were two regiments of white illiterates at this Training Center. There are boys of superior intelligence, boys of normal abilities, and others. Likewise, there have come boys who have had the finest background of religious training and experience, and those with little or no religious training. There are men of many faiths, men of much faith, and men of little faith. Their sudden change of circumstances and environment is a crucial test and may prove to be a severe test for the faith that is in them.

The religious preference of 74.7 per cent of the men (white) who passed through this largest naval training center in the world in the year 1944 was Protestant; 23 per cent were Roman Catholic; 1.7 per cent were Jewish. The religious preference of 93.8 per cent of the Negroes was Protestant, of 6 per cent was Roman Catholic. Professing atheists (White or Negro) were quite rare—perhaps not one in a thousand.

IV

What do these lads bring with them from the outside world of bobby-socks and boogie-woogie? Many of them enlisted before their eighteenth birthday. They may have barely completed high school. They may never have attended high school. How well are they equipped to stand up to life? How well are they prepared to stand alone, without father or mother near by? Yesterday they were boys—mere children; today they are setting out on the great adventure—to complete the biggest and toughest job in the history of the world.

It is extremely difficult to determine the main level of moral and spiritual standards and to describe the vague religious beliefs of boys, seventeen to twenty, who come into the Navy by enlistment or induction. And, of course, anyone who is so rash as to attempt such an appraisal makes himself a target for all who observe youth from other levels and from different angles. It is possible to find in the raw recruit just about anything that is sought. However, it is far more difficult to find the mean level of moral and spiritual standards than it is to determine the average intelligence. The recruit is subjected to nine tests, in order to discover his intelligence, fitness, and aptitude. No such tests are available for studying his moral and spiritual level. The most that can be set down here is the result of the very limited knowledge and observation of one person with the assistance of some of his associates in the Chaplains' Department at this Center. Recruits, individually and collectively, facts and figures, must tell as much as possible.

The raw recruit brings with him a taste for comics which he prefers above all other magazines. Next to these, he likes joke books and cartoon books. These are followed by monthly and weekly picture magazines, featuring popular show girls and dancers. The list continues with more substantial material, including the digests. Western and detective stories take their places after these, followed in order by movie magazines, sports magazines, and crossword puzzles.

The total circulation of books issued from the Center Library, including eleven branch libraries, for the year 1944 was 211,629. Of course, the demand for fiction was far out in front. Current best-sellers and westerns topped the list. Of nonfiction, books in the various fields of applied science and useful arts were requested most. Other classifications in the order of their demand were as follows: world history, literature, biography, military and naval sciences, social sciences, travel, fine arts, philosophy, and religion.

The average recruit brings with him some admirable traits and qualities. His power to adapt himself to new situations is remarkable. But whatever else the average recruit brings with him into the Navy, he brings very little interest in religion and in spiritual values. He brings with him very little knowledge of the Bible and of religious literature, even though he may have attended Sunday School a good part of his life. He may not even know the two main divisions of the Bible. He can name but a few books of the Bible. He may not be able to name any favorite Old Testament character. He may name Samson, or Abraham, Joseph, Moses, David, Daniel, or Job; but he is not always able to say exactly why.

The average recruit knows that Jesus died on the cross. He is not sure of his age at the time of his death. He may not know, or he may give it as anywhere between thirty and thirty-eight, or seventy. The mere mention of the Sermon on the Mount brings no response. It is even confused with the life of Moses. The parables of Jesus are little known to the average recruit. Mention of miracles draws hardly an answer. The Lord's prayer is, perhaps, best known. However, there are many who cannot repeat it without help. Words of the Christian Faith—sacrament, communion, grace, prayer, baptism, creed, commandments —convey very little meaning to the average raw recruit, and draw no clear statement.

The average recruit is indifferent toward expressions of religion and toward forms of spiritual interest. He would not of his own accord leave his barracks and cross the street to hear the most outstanding preacher in the country. He has not the slightest desire to join a group for the purpose of studying the Bible or anything else in his spare time. Neither would he make any effort to hear a good concert. He might work up some enthusiasm for a hot jam session. There are those who do not care for this, either.

While it is true that the average recruit would not make the slightest effort to attend church individually and of his own accord, it is also true that if the rest of his company, or most of his company, falls in for church, he will fall in, too. If divine service is in the plan of the day, he will take it as a matter of course, and may even become interested in it. An order from the Secretary of the Navy forbids compulsory attendance at church.

Jesse Stuart, author of "Taps for Private Tussie," went through Recruit Training as an apprentice seaman at this Center in April–May 1944. He is one who can be depended upon to know and to be straightforward in presenting the reactions of the people with whom he lives. Asked what the men of his company thought of divine service at Great Lakes, he said that they took it seriously and were pleased to have it in the regular Sunday schedule. There were, no doubt, other views and unfavorable attitudes; but, in general, Stuart's testimony has been borne out by most companies in recruit training. When the National Preaching Mission of the Federal Council of Churches of Christ in America visited the Center in October 1944, one out of every five men who were interviewed by a visiting clergyman stated that he had not been interested in a church service until he came to Great Lakes. On completion of recruit training many have felt that their religious life has been strengthened by the divine services held at this Center.

If they know the hymns, they will join in singing. However, there are relatively few hymns that are known to all. With the words before them they come out well in the Lord's Prayer, in the creed, and in responsive readings. They will listen to the sermon if the chaplain has something to say and if he says it in an effective way. If they can find a comfortable position, some will doze or "dope off" (go woolgathering). However, it is possible to keep them awake and to hold their sustained interest throughout. It takes an extraordinary sermon and a forceful delivery to do it, but it can be done, and it has been done. It's a workout for the chaplain, but it's worth the effort.

One of the things which must be constantly kept in mind is that the average recruit knows less of the Bible and of literature in general, to say nothing of philosophy and other subjects, than is often assumed. One criticism which may be made of most sermons is that these are over the heads of most men. Anyone who preaches to recruits and who wanders off into the abstract will find his congregation suddenly taking on the appearance of a cornfield after hail or a windstorm has passed through that part of the country. Instead of nice even rows with heads up, he will find the most grotesque expressions, shapes, and patterns before him. On the other hand, it is not at all necessary to resort to the sensational, nor to wise-cracking, nor to stories or language which are out of character. The average recruit will sit up and take notice and respond to something that he can understand, if it is presented in such a way as to awaken and hold his interest.

On one occasion I spoke to 1200 men in Building X. These men were still in civilian clothes, having arrived within the previous thirty-six hours. I spoke on "Faith for a Man of Action," using the Apostle Paul's great testimony to Timothy (II Timothy 1:12): "For I know whom I have believed, and am persuaded that he is able to keep that which I have committed unto him against that day." I suggested that this would be a good verse for them to mark in their New Testaments. It might serve them well. I added that if they did not have copies of the New Testament, these would be given to them if they would come forward after the service. Three hundred and sixty-three men came forward after the service to receive New Testaments. Many requested help in finding the text in II Timothy.

New Testaments and Psalms are made available to men in Recruit Training through the coöperation of the American Bible Society and The Gideons with the chaplains. These are distributed each Sunday after each divine service (Protestant) to men who come forward to receive them. In the year 1944 the total number of New Testaments distributed in this way and in chaplains' offices throughout the Training Center at Great Lakes was 188,152.

Attendance at divine service is a new experience for some recruits. There are those who are members of churches and who have attended regularly; there are others who have been irregular in attendance; still others have rarely gone to church, and some not at all. A young recruit applied at a chaplain's office for instruction preparatory to baptism. He claimed to know nothing of his parents, having been left at the age of six months on the doorstep of a prospector in the Southwest. When he was about twelve years old, the prospector disappeared. His childhood and youth were spent prospecting and ranching. He told of sleeping on the ground with no shelter but that provided by a lariat which was laid out in a circle around him to discourage the lizards and the rattlesnakes from coming too close. He said that he

had been in many states and that he was tending elephants
for Ringling Brothers at the time of the tragic fire in Hart-
ford, Connecticut, early in July 1944. He claimed to have
assisted in saving the lives of some of the children from
the flaming canvas. He said that when he was sixteen he
killed a Mexican in self-defense. A drunken man had reeled
into him. Sensing the situation, the lad apologized. The
Mexican, thinking the boy was swearing at him, slashed at
the lad with a knife, cutting his arm. The youngster pulled
a gun and shot him. At least, this was his story in reply to
certain questions asked by the chaplain. He displayed the
scar on his arm.

This recruit had had little or no formal education, but
was alert and observing. Unable to produce a birth cer-
tificate, he was not accepted for enlistment at Navy Recruiting Stations. Finally, he appealed to the F.B.I. in
Washington, D. C., and was assured that if he really wanted
to get into the Navy, he would be given all the assistance
required.

Attendance at divine service each Sunday in recruit training gave him the desire to be baptized. He had had no
religious instruction before. Here was a lad whose first
experience of religion occurred in the Navy.

More than a thousand men were baptized by Protestant
chaplains at Great Lakes in the year 1944. More than three
hundred were baptized by Roman Catholic chaplains. The
number of men confirmed in the Roman Catholic faith was
960. Every effort is made to unite the men, Protestant,

Roman Catholic, Jewish, or Christian Science, with the churches in their own communities.

Personal interviews of chaplains with men (chiefly recruits) at this Center numbered 118,450 for the past year. These interviews concerned all sorts of personal matters and problems. It is estimated that approximately ten per cent of the interviews were on matters essentially religious. Others dealt with questions of all sorts. There were family problems and emergencies, involving referral to the Navy Relief Society and the American Red Cross. There were many interviews regarding human relationships of one kind or another. These may appear to be anything but religious. However, in counseling it is frequently helpful to reach into the religious background of the individual for what assistance may be needed.

Chaplains who announce at their Sunday morning services that they will be in their offices Sunday afternoon find many callers. Chaplains are also available in their offices on weekdays in the late afternoon and evening when recruits are at leisure. Interviews with recruits reveal emotional reactions to their absence from home, and the difficulties of adjusting to a strange environment and of learning to live with a cross section of men in the same barracks. In some cases, interviews reveal uneasiness with regard to the ability of the individual to measure up to certain standards and to fulfill the requirements. Occasionally a man comes in and expresses grave doubts that he will have the physical courage necessary to perform the duties expected of him.

He seems to be reassured when he is told that, when his big moment comes, he will be so busy doing the thing that needs to be done that there will be no time for fear. The average recruit, however, seems to work out his own salvation in silence, even though there may be fear and trembling within him. He soon learns to keep his eyes and ears open and his mouth shut, and to volunteer for nothing.

The raw recruit responds readily to training, even though he may find stretches of washboard road. His big asset is willingness to learn. He makes mistakes for which due allowance is made. The need for disciplinary action in recruit training is at a minimum. The individual recruit finds his life made simpler by regimentation. He does not have to plan his day; it is all arranged for him. He is kept too busy to allow any time for self-pity. What if he does get only two hours' sleep because of a midwatch? His training will be over in a few weeks. He learns to grin and bear it. He learns also to take a lot of heckling. He learns to dish it out, too.

v

It has been the custom at this Center to hold Communion Services in connection with the regularly scheduled Protestant services on the first Sunday of each month. On each Communion Sunday, from six to ten thousand have elected to remain and to join in the Communion Services throughout the Center. Of every thousand men of Protestant faith who attended church at Great Lakes in the year 1944, those who remained to receive Communion numbered 227.

In order to accommodate all hands, Protestant services have been scheduled at 8.15, 9.30, and 10.45 each Sunday morning in each drill hall in recruit areas; while at the same time Roman Catholic Masses, Jewish and Christian Science services, have been held in recreation buildings. It can readily be seen that with such a time table, in order to serve Communion to several hundred men at each of the three services in each of the drill halls, arrangements must be worked out very carefully. The intinction form of Communion has been found most acceptable. Communicants approach the Communion rail and kneel to receive the bread (wafer) dipped in the chalice.

There are those who will always prefer the Communion Service after the manner to which they were accustomed at home. However, there are many who find the Communion Services at Great Lakes very helpful and impressive, even though the form is different from the one to which they have been accustomed. Some who have evidently received the elements in seated position in their own churches have expressed themselves as particularly impressed by kneeling at the Communion rail which they first learned at Great Lakes. Side by side at the Communion rail kneel men of all Christian faiths. The Lutheran is not at all disturbed to receive Communion from a Presbyterian chaplain, nor is he at all concerned that the man kneeling at one side of him is a Baptist or that the man on the other side is a Methodist. The next man may genuflect as he leaves the Communion rail.

Communion Services are held for Episcopalians, Lutherans, Roman Catholics, and others each Sunday of the month and on weekdays as requested, and whenever possible.

VI

Any discussion of "The Faith and Practice of the Raw Recruit" is incomplete without the view mirrored by the Great Lakes Bluejacket Choir. Starting with a group of twenty men in 1941, the volunteer membership has expanded with the Center into a service organization numbering more than one thousand men in active participation each Sunday. On no two Sundays is the choir personnel exactly the same. As men complete their training and move on, new recruits take their places. Each man sings with the choir not over nine weeks, when the recruit training period is ten weeks. When the recruit training period was five weeks, men were in the choir approximately one month before moving on.

In order to facilitate rehearsal periods and movement of troops, when the rate of induction was highest, choir companies were formed. A company of a hundred and twenty to a hundred and thirty men consisted entirely of choir members who received their recruit training as a unit. These choir companies won many "roosters"—high honors awarded for smart military performance. It was an inspiration never to be forgotten to hear one of the choir companies suddenly burst into four-part harmony as it marched along.

Choir companies have been replaced by regimental choirs. As each incoming company is formed in the Receiving Regiment, a motion picture is exhibited, giving a preview of the life which may be expected in recruit training. Immediately following the picture, a specialist (W) (choir director) from the Chaplains' Department gives a brief talk regarding the choir. Men who are interested remain for quick tryouts. An average of one out of every six incoming recruits is interested in trying out for the choir. Of those who try out, one out of every eight is Roman Catholic, and one out of every forty is Jewish. The rest are Protestants. The director of the Roman Catholic Choir attributes the dearth of singers available for his choir to several main factors, i.e., lack of musical training in parochial schools, very limited congregational singing, and very limited participation in choirs of Roman Catholic churches.

Certain trends may be traced geographically in the selection of men for the choir. As companies are formed, the recruits from area drafts usually become members of the same unit. It has been found that in groups originating from the middle-western states more men are interested in choral work, and more men are capable of doing good choral work, than those from the southern or eastern states. Exceptions may be found in certain communities, but the general trend has been found as stated.

The records reveal that men in choirs have attained unusually high marks in service school entrance examinations.

Choir companies averaged more than ninety per cent of personnel qualified for advanced training. In three choir companies, every man was assigned to a service school.

At the present time, seven men from each company of a hundred and twenty men are permitted to join the choir. This number includes Roman Catholics as well as Protestants. Men trained in the Great Lakes Bluejacket Choir in the year 1944 numbered 7100. Approximately 20,000 men have been trained in the choir since early in 1941. The choir sings as a unit (1000 men) on special occasions such as a radio program on Navy Day, carols on Christmas eve, a special program over four networks on the occasion of the President's Birthday Celebration for the National Foundation for Infantile Paralysis. Otherwise, it comprises eighteen choirs, the largest of which, a Protestant choir, consists of a hundred and fifty men. There are eleven Protestant choirs, six Roman Catholic choirs, and one Jewish choir. All of these provide special music for two or three services and for a radio program over an international network each Sunday morning.

As may be expected, men in the choirs are on the whole better coördinated physically, mentally, morally, and spiritually than the average. They have had better than average religious background. There is a more concentrated sprinkling of ministers' sons.

Letters are received at the choir office from men in all parts of the world recalling their pleasant associations with the choir. They get together and tune up in ships of the fleet. A certain small destroyer which carries no chaplain has an active choir, nevertheless. A group of men got together and gave a concert under the name of the Great Lakes Bluejacket Choir in one of the cathedrals in Scotland. A troop train carrying men from Great Lakes to the West Coast was delayed at a small railroad station in the desert on a Sunday morning. The men assembled on the railway platform for a brief service of worship. The officer in charge of the draft read a selection from the New Testament. There were sufficient members of the choir to render several anthems and to lead in the singing of hymns. Men who have sung in the choir at Great Lakes carry away with them memories and impressions which they will never forget. The words of certain hymns and anthems will stay with them for years.

VII

No statistics are available as to the personal habits of the raw recruit which may throw light upon his moral standards. It is easy to generalize from surface indications without considering all aspects. The uncouth members of any group of men often sound off first and loudest, and may appear to set the standard for the entire group at a rather low level. In the same group, there are others who, in the absence of the refining and restraining influences of mothers, wives, and sisters, and with the desire to appear rugged and virile, begin to vie with the boorish and the boisterous. Those who have been reared in a religious

environment and who find themselves suddenly confronted
with such an entirely different situation may become per-
plexed and alarmed.

Recently there was a telephone call from one of the
farthest camps in Greenbay, sometimes referred to at Great
Lakes as "Siberia." The man was anxious to talk to a Protestant chaplain. When he was assured that he was speaking
to a Protestant chaplain, he said,

Sir, I need your help. I hope you will do something for
me. I am an ordained minister, twenty-seven years old, I
enlisted in the Navy, thinking that I could be a blessing to
these boys. But, Sir, it's so different from what I expected.
I have something in my heart, just as you have. I have a
church back home, and I feel that I can do more for the
Lord back there than I can here. I didn't know it would be
like this. Will you please help me to get out of the Navy?
And, Sir, do you think you can get me out before they cut
my hair?

Nostalgia and a strong antipathy for life in a barracks with
men whom he could not understand and who did not ap-
preciate his views made him of all men most miserable.

Raw recruits bring with them into the Naval service
habits of speech and habits of life which are disturbing to
the uninitiated and to the more sensitive. However, any
man who is well grounded in his faith, and any man who
has ideals and high standards of personal conduct may
carry these with him wherever he goes. Within the physical
limits of his new environment, he may, nevertheless, continue to live his own personal and spiritual life, and he is

respected accordingly. The influence and power of a good man is nowhere more quickly observed nor more fully appreciated than in the Navy.

It was one of the most refreshing experiences to meet a tall, blond, curly-haired boy of nineteen. He was an ordained minister, but enlisted in the Navy in order to do his share in the war effort. He would have liked to serve as a chaplain, but, with only two years of college, his educational qualifications were not sufficient, and so he was quite willing to bear a hand where he could best serve. In recruit training, his company commander was pleased to have him conduct an informal service in the barracks. It brought the men closer together, and promoted a fine spirit in the company, according to the man in charge.

The men admired and respected the lad. He spoke well, and they knew he believed what he said. His simple directness without obtrusiveness attracted men to him. He impressed them with his manner, as well as by his speech. When he broke out his New Testament in the evening, others found it easier to do likewise. Some would drift over to his bunk and compare readings. Discussion of various subjects relating to the Christian religion and to things in general frequently followed.

When the company had completed training and was about to shove off on recruit leave, there were those who were especially indebted to this youth. The quiet power of his influence and example had brought out the best in them. Life was somehow different for having known the lad from Oklahoma.

In a few of the companies, men have spontaneously formed groups for brief devotions in the barracks a little while before taps. Some of these groups have comprised large parts of their companies. Men of different faiths have taken turns in reading passages from the New Testament or Psalms and leading in prayer, all joining in the Lord's Prayer.

VIII

The recruit may define God as "Creator and Ruler of the universe," "Divine Person in control of life," "a Sacred Person to be feared and loved," or "Someone we can turn to for help." He may not even attempt a definition. It is curious to observe, however, that more are able and willing to give some idea of God than of human characters in the Bible. The faith of the average recruit is inchoate and inarticulate. It was imparted to him in Sunday School and by contact with others. He has no adequate words for it, any more than he has for love or loyalty or friendship.

The practice of the raw recruit may leave something to be desired. Viewed from the lofty heights of the teachings of Jesus, the moral standards of men in the mass may not appear to be at a very high level. As individuals, the best of men fall far short of the mark of the high calling. Jesus did not enter into judgment of anyone taken in sin. There is no attempt here to enter into judgment of any man or of any group of men. The average recruit is no different from the rest of the youth of our land. He has instincts and appetites, dispositions and impulses which at times may throw him for a loss.

Whatever the average level may be, there is a considerable element among recruits which makes no great display, but which carries on with a high sense of religious and moral values. There are men with the finest ideals regarding life in general and marriage in particular. It is too early for many of them to consider marriage, but they have high standards and high hopes.

IX

The average recruit will do well the job that he has come into the Navy to finish. He will do this well, because he will be well trained and well equipped. If and when he goes into action, he will be prepared to react to various situations. He will be prepared to carry out orders and instructions. If decisions are required of him, these will be made largely on the basis of his training and experience in the naval service. In the midst of an engagement, he will be so busy doing the thing that needs to be done and which he has been trained to do that he will not think of what may happen to him. In fact, he will probably be more aware of what is happening to others than of what is happening to himself. He will be more concerned for others than he is for himself. When the commanding officer of a submarine in the Pacific suddenly found himself in the range of enemy guns and gave the order, "Take her down," he was doing the thing that he was trained to do. He had been wounded and the minutes required to carry him below would have increased the peril to his ship and crew. His order cost him his life, but saved his ship and crew. In critical situations and in other situations, men react according to their training.

The war could not be won without the indispensable assistance of men who have in recent months and years been average recruits. These men have gone out and will continue to go forth to perform the duties for which they are trained. Many of these have distinguished themselves by unusual performance of duty, because they were on hand at a critical moment and because they did the things that they were trained to do. The training period for many has not been long—a few months—at most, a few years.

In the first seventeen years of his life, what has the church done to instruct, train, and equip the average recruit for the major battles which confront every youth as he approaches manhood? What has the church done to prepare boys to live in barracks with a cross section of American youth? What has the church done to enable the lad to make good selections and choices in changing circumstances and environment? What has the church done to train the young man to make good decisions? What has the church done to condition the youth for the race that is set before him? What has the church done to help the boy stand on his own feet away from home without being too easily misled? What has the church done to season him for the give-and-take of recruit training and of Navy life in general? What has the church done to strengthen his moral fiber to resist all sorts of temptation which confront him on liberty in a strange city or in a foreign port? What has the church done to give him a taste for and an interest in things that are of good report? What has the church done to prepare him for life at sea and beyond the sea? What has the church done to provide him with inner resources for the endless hours of inaction? What has the church done to equip him for mortal combat? What has the church done to reinforce him for desperate situations unforeseen? What has the church done to prepare him to live? What has the church done to prepare him to die? What has the church done to enable him to face and to endure pain and suffering? What has the church done to preserve in youth, even while he is engaged in the great struggle, the things for which he is fighting, the things for which he is risking his life, the things for which he is giving his life? What has the church done to prevent the young veteran, when he returns, from losing through his own limitations, neglect, and indifference the things for which he has given so much?

Let the church search its own soul for the answers to these questions. It may not be important to know the two main divisions of the Bible or the books of the Bible, or even the Sermon on the Mount or the parables. However, lack of this knowledge indicates a far more serious condition. If the church has not provided these simplest elements, what has it done with regard to the great issues of life? We are not unmindful of the many efforts that have been made by the church in behalf of youth, nor do we overlook the many efforts that are being made by the church in behalf of men and women in the armed forces. However, too many of these have been too little and, particularly, too late. As members and servants of the church, we chaplains share in the soul-searching that is needed.

Our concept of freedom may need some reëxamining in some of its departments. We are anxious to have our children reared with opportunity for the most complete self-expression and for the fullest exercise of freedom. Yet we do insist upon their learning the three R's and a few other things. We take definite steps to prevent them from becoming intellectual morons. What steps are taken to prevent them from becoming moral and spiritual morons? Our interpretation of religious freedom includes freedom to be irreligious. To be irreligious may mean that one is merely disregardful of religion; or, according to the dictionary, it may mean that one is profane, which signifies contempt for religion on a descending scale. Is it any wonder that parents who are disregardful of religion may find their children profane and contemptuous of religion? Many good and otherwise intelligent people agree that Sunday School is a fine thing for children, but they don't insist upon their children attending regularly; and when the children reach the age of twelve, they frequently discontinue entirely, unless the parents are sufficiently interested themselves to attend. If the church were more generally awake to the tremendous issues involved, the leaders would take the Sunday School more seriously, provide the best instruction possible, at whatever cost, including visual aid, and round up the children, impressing upon the parents that it is a "must" for the community. If the church does not provide adequate youth centers—adequate in every sense of the word—youth will find his interests elsewhere.

A local clergyman who has entertained thousands of bluejackets at Sunday dinners has been impressed with their reactions toward the church schedule at Great Lakes. Many have assured him that they have found a new and vital interest in religion. They approved wholeheartedly its inclusion in the regular training program. One of the bluejackets was asked what he would do if he had teen-aged sons and daughters; would he compel them to attend Sunday School or church? He replied that he would use all of his powers of persuasion first; but he would see that they went.

If it is true that, in critical situations and in other situations, men react according to their training, let the church have greater regard for the handwriting on the wall, and let it give more serious attention to the training of childhood and youth. It may not be the church's function to regiment young men in barracks; but it is the church's function to indoctrinate its youth in such a thorough understanding and appreciation of moral and spiritual values that life in any barracks with the roughest and toughest of men will not prove too great a strain. It may not be the church's function to teach and to encourage men to kill; but it is the church's function and duty to undergird a man with such a faith and with such an understanding of the issues involved that he will be able to accomplish what is expected of him by his God and by his country.

NOTE. The opinions or assertions contained herein are the private ones of the writer and are not to be construed as official or reflecting the views of the Navy Department or of the naval service at large.

⊹ *4* ⊹

The Ministry of the Chaplain

THE chaplains of our Armed Forces are all volunteers. The Selective Service Act specifically exempts from military service all duly ordained ministers of religion. Yet from the very earliest days the people of America have recognized the need of a vital religious program in the Army and Navy. The chaplaincy in the United States Army and Navy began during the Revolutionary War when clergymen were assigned to brigade headquarters of the Continental Army and frigates of the fleet. The Act of March 3, 1791 fixed the strength of the Army at 2232 officers and men and provided for the appointment of a chaplain. The first known Navy chaplain was appointed in 1778 and served aboard the Frigates *Boston* and *Alliance*. He was the Reverend Benjamin Balch, who fought at Lexington with the famous "Minute Men" and served as an Army chaplain in Colonel Ephraim Doolittle's regiment before he entered the Naval services. With the exception of a few brief periods in the early 1800's, there have been chaplains in the Army and Navy from that day to this. They have served on the battlefields of all our wars. They have sailed the Seven Seas with the fleet. They have lived in lonely army posts on the Western Frontier; they have served in the Canal Zone, and Hawaii, and China, and the Philippines, and Alaska. They are serving today in ships and stations and on battle fronts literally all over the world.

Before the present emergency there were about 150 chaplains in the Army and 80 chaplains in the Navy. Today there are about 7800 chaplains in the Army and 2400 in the Navy. How were these additional chaplains obtained? Besides the Reserve Corps officers of both the Army and Navy and National Guard chaplains who were called to active duty, great numbers of clergymen with no previous contact with military life volunteered "for the duration of the emergency and six months thereafter."

Not every volunteer was accepted. Each applicant for the chaplaincy must present an ecclesiastical endorsement from his own denomination. He must meet the educational standards of college and seminary training required by existing regulations. He must pass the same physical test that is required of a line officer.

The chaplains are drawn from more than fifty different religious groups in numbers proportionate to the strength of the denomination which they represent. The ratio has had to be altered in a few cases, when a denomination has

been unable to meet its quota, but in general it can be said
that the chaplains of the Army and Navy form a cross section of the religious life of America. They are Catholic,
Protestant, and Jewish. They are white and black and yel-
low. There is a Japanese Christian chaplain serving a battalion of Japanese-American troops with a splendid battle
record in Italy. They are from every state in the Union
and from every great national strain that has become a part
of the varied and colorful pattern of American life.

II

Both the Army and Navy recognized the necessity of
training newly appointed chaplains for their task. There
was no thought of teaching them theology or the conduct
of public worship. They had been appointed because they
had already the necessary professional training and experience. But it was necessary to teach them the ways of the
Services and to help them adapt their ministry to the peculiar conditions of Army and Navy life.

The Army Chaplain School was reactivated and began
its work at Fort Benjamin Harrison in March 1942. In August 1942 it was moved to Harvard University and in
August 1944 to Fort Devens, Massachusetts. The course is
five weeks in length. The basic subject is Practical Duties of
the Chaplain. Other subjects are Military Discipline, Cour-
tesies and Customs, Army Morale, Army Organization,
Army Administration, Military Sanitation, First Aid,
Graves Registration, Military Law, Map Reading, and De-

fense Against Chemical Warfare. There are hours of close order drill and calisthenics. Since the transfer of the School to Fort Devens there has been a period of amphibious landing training, across the waters of a little lake, and an afternoon on the infiltration course, crawling under barbed wire, under live ammunition. There are also daily devotional services for each of the three major faiths.

As the war passed into its third year, more and more chaplains who had been sent overseas in the days immediately after Pearl Harbor without attending the School were being brought back on rotation or because of physical disability. These chaplains were ordered to the School for a refresher course and have, by their presence, done much to enrich the life of the School.

The Navy Chaplain School was organized at Norfolk, Virginia, in February 1942, and in March 1943 moved to William and Mary College, Williamsburg, Virginia. The Navy course is eight weeks in length, of which two weeks are employed in a "shake-down" cruise, when students are assigned to duty under supervision of chaplains at Naval installations. In addition to the "cruise," once a week throughout the course students make field trips to explore some phase of the many Naval activities in the vicinity— the Navy Yard at Portsmouth, the Naval Air Station, the Naval Operating Base at Norfolk, or one of the many Coast Guard and Marine Corps units in that area. The Naval School also prepares its students for the recreational, athletic, and social service activities that may be a part of their duties.

III

The chaplain's duties in either the Army or the Navy are primarily those of a minister of religion. There is an almost unbelievable variety in the type of assignment possible in time of war. A Navy chaplain may be assigned to a training ship in New York Harbor and hold services every Sunday in Riverside Church. Or he may be attached to a Marine regiment and go ashore at Tarawa, or serve on a capital ship on any one of the Seven Seas. He may serve with a Naval construction battalion (Seabees) or ashore or afloat with men of the Coast Guard. An Army chaplain may be in a training center in the United States or on a fog-bound island in the Aleutians or with troops in any one of a dozen theaters of operations. He may ride his caboose on the railways of the Persian Gulf Command or serve in a hospital or on a transport. It is impossible to describe the work of any one man and say, "This is a typical chaplain."

There is just one bond that unites all the chaplains of all faiths and in all situations into a single brotherhood. That is the bond of religious devotion. Whatever may be the particular requirements of their special assignment, every true chaplain is first of all a man of God.

The duties of a chaplain are indicated in statements made by Chaplain William R. Arnold, Chief of Chaplains of the Army, and by Chaplain Robert D. Workman, Chief Chaplain of the Navy.[1]

---

[1] "The Chaplaincy in the Armed Forces," *Army and Navy Journal,* 7 December 1944.

Chaplain Arnold writes:

What has actually been done by chaplains in this war cannot be measured exactly. It cannot be named detail by detail. The religious ideal incorporated into their pledge, to render spiritual aid, comfort and guidance, to provide religious services and ministrations for military personnel, and to build and maintain character is recognized even by the unreligious as one of the most important facts in military morale.

Chaplain Workman writes:

Because a chaplain's duties are primarily religious, our chaplains' foremost concern is that a man shall be prepared spiritually for any eventuality. We would substitute for the more popular slogan, "No atheists in fox holes," the more realistic one which contends that "the fox hole is a poor place for a man to begin to learn how to pray." Chaplains have enough evidence from combat zones to present a convincing argument which favors spiritual preparation before a man is forced to look down an enemy gun barrel.

The Army chaplain is a member of the staff of the commanding officer of the unit to which he is assigned. He is the logical consultant of the commanding officer in all matters relating to religion, morals, and morale. Army regulations specifically direct that he shall not be required to perform secular duties which might interfere with his function as a minister of religion. For example, the Army chaplain will not be placed in charge of the sports or recreational activities of his unit. He will not be in charge of educational work or social service. He will not serve as Defense Counsel in a Court Martial or as War Bond Officer or Insurance Officer. All of these activities are necessary to the efficiency of the Army. They must be done by someone; but they are not primarily religious and hence they will not be done by the chaplain. More than at any previous period in our Army's history, the War Department recognizes the unique function of the chaplain. The religious work which he is specifically appointed to accomplish cannot be done by any other officer in the Army. If the chaplain is not free to do it, it will not be done. Hence, present regulations make every effort to protect the chaplain from any assignment which would interfere with the religious ministry which originally led him into the Army.

Army Regulations specifically place responsibility for the religious program of a unit upon the commanding officer. One regulation reads:

Chaplains are required by law to conduct appropriate religious services for the commands to which they are assigned. Commanders must give these activities due share of their attention and must insure the effectiveness of their performance by rendering every practicable aid to chaplains. In order that military personnel may be free to attend such services as they may desire, commanders will reduce military duty and labor on Sunday to the measure of strict necessity. Such duties as are required by the military situation and any athletic or recreational activities that may be held on Sunday will, if practicable, be so scheduled as not to interfere with attendance on services of worship.

Another reads:

To facilitate compliance with the regulations which direct chaplains to hold appropriate religious services for the benefit of the commands to which they are assigned, it will be the duty of commanding officers to afford chaplains serving under them such available facilities as may aid them in the performance of their duties and to detail such needed assistants to chaplains as may be deemed desirable and practicable by commanding officers. It shall be the duty of the post or garrison commander to set apart a suitable room or building for school and religious purposes. Authorization will be given for such publicity for chaplain activities through official channels as the need may warrant.

The duties of a Navy chaplain differ somewhat from the Army chaplain in that he may be assigned certain miscellaneous duties in addition to the religious services, the visitation of the sick, conferences, and consultations. Additional tasks may include assisting in the educational, entertainment, and welfare program, and supervising ship and station libraries.

The Articles of Government of the Navy, like Army Regulations, place responsibility for the religious program of a ship or station upon the commanding officer. The articles read:

The commander of vessels and naval stations to which chaplains are attached shall cause divine service to be performed on Sunday whenever the weather or other circumstances allow it to be done.

In order to insure the regular performance of divine services aboard the vessels of the United States Navy and at shore stations, it is further ordered that in no instance shall secular work be allowed to interfere with the holding of divine services and that every possible assistance and encouragement be given to chaplains in the conduct of such services. A suitable compartment or room shall be designated for this purpose and properly rigged for the occasion and orderly quiet be maintained throughout the ship during divine services.

When there is no chaplain attached to his ship or station, the commanding officer will arrange for and give every possible assistance to any Naval chaplain in squadron or available who might be able to come aboard for such purpose. In case it is impossible to secure the services of a regular Navy chaplain, it is directed that commanding officers, when practicable, invite competent clergymen from ashore to come aboard and conduct religious services.

IV

The first and most obvious duty of the chaplain is to conduct public religious services for the personnel of the unit to which he is assigned and to provide services for men of other faiths to whom he is not qualified to minister. The services held by either an Army or Navy chaplain will be very like the services he held in civilian life modified only by the necessities of the military situation.

For the Catholic soldier or sailor, as for the Catholic in civilian life, it is the Mass that matters. The Roman Catholic chaplain has been given permission to hold evening Masses, beginning as late as 7.30 P. M. Day after day, on ships at sea, in garrison and in the field, on transports, in hospitals and Reception Centers, and in every Army and Navy installation, the daily Mass calls forth its thousands of worshipers.

Holy Communion usually is made available to Protestant personnel at least once each month. The chaplain also performs baptisms and marriages and conducts burial services much as would a minister in civilian life. A man who seeks baptism or who makes a first profession of faith is urged and encouraged by the chaplain to relate himself to a parish or congregation back home.

Services seldom are more than forty-five minutes long. Hence, the sermon itself seldom lasts more than twelve or fifteen minutes. As one chaplain, ripe in wisdom and experience, has said, "Long sermons are out for the duration and six months thereafter." It may even be that the habits of brevity inculcated by experience in the chaplaincy will be carried over into the civilian ministry to the edification of hundreds of congregations!

The chaplain soon learns that a short sermon demands more careful preparation than a long sermon. He learns in preaching to tired, sleepy men to be clear, concise, and definite. If he is wise, he learns that men facing loneliness and death are not interested in good advice about the details of conduct. What they want are the great affirmations of religious faith stated simply and convincingly by a man whose own life and faith speak louder than any mere words. Men want to believe that there is a God and that God cares. They want to know that the Divine love watches over their families thousands of miles away and over them in all the dangers of battle. They want to believe in a God great enough and good enough to take care of them in this life and in the life beyond. The chaplain who can bring to men these living beliefs of religion will never fail to find officers and men ready to listen.

Month after month the Office of the Chief of Chaplains of the Army issues its figures of attendance upon services of worship. The month of September 1944 is typical:

Number of Religious Services	131,037
Total Attendance	7,643,240
Number Receiving Communion	816,973

The Office of the Chief of Chaplains has prepared a chart that shows the rising trend of the religious life of the Army from July 1941 to May 1944. The chart shows that the number of chaplains increased by 546 per cent; the number of services increased by 830 per cent; attendance upon services increased by 871 per cent; and the number of men who received Holy Communion increased by 1549 per cent. In the Navy, corresponding increases in attendance are indicated by chaplains' annual reports. We not only have more chaplains in the Army and Navy, but the average chaplain is working harder and his efforts are calling forth a wider response.

Few chaplains believe that there is any widespread revival of religion taking place in the Armed Forces. Yet, the actual figures seem to be more optimistic than the offhand impression of the chaplains themselves. Surely it is significant that by far the highest rate of increase is in the number of servicemen, both Catholic and Protestant, who receive Holy Communion. Nor is it the case that this is what has sometimes been rather cynically called "fox hole religion" —the religion of a frightened man which evaporates into thin air the moment danger is removed. It is true that attendance upon services usually is better as a unit approaches the front. Surely there is nothing unworthy in a man, face to face with one of the supreme experiences of life, seeking the aid of a Power greater than himself. The test of the sincerity of religion at the front is found when a unit comes out of the lines into a rest area. Again and again, reports have shown a continued interest in religion and a continued attendance upon services after the pressure of extreme and imminent danger has been removed.

In the Army a typical program of religious services for a week will run something like this:

CATHOLIC SERVICES

Sundays

Masses	7 and 11 A. M.
Benediction	7 P. M.

Weekdays

Masses	Mondays, Wednesdays, and Fridays at 7 P. M.
Masses	Tuesdays, Thursdays, and Saturdays at 6 A. M.
Instruction	Wednesdays at 7.45 P. M.
Confessions	Saturdays from 4 to 6 and from 7 to 10 P. M.

PROTESTANT SERVICES

Sundays

Episcopal Holy Communion 1st and 3rd Sundays at 9 A. M.
Lutheran Holy Communion 2nd and 4th Sundays at 9 A. M.
Worship and Sermon   10 A. M.
Song Service   8 P. M.

Weekdays

Bible Class   Tuesdays at 7 P. M.
Prayer Service   Thursdays at 7 P. M.
Choir Rehearsal   Thursdays at 8 P. M.

Christian Science Service Tuesdays at 8 P. M.

JEWISH SERVICES

Fridays   8 P. M.

On Naval establishments ashore the weekly religious service would approximate the above. Afloat, in the Navy:

On most ships of the fleet, divine service is held at ten o'clock each Sunday. First indication is the bugler sounding over the ship's loudspeaker system "Church Call," followed by the voice of the boatswain's mate of the watch admonishing all that "The smoking lamp is out, knock off all card games, turn off all radios, keep silence about the decks during the divine service." The ship's bell tolls the summons to worship, the National Colors are then dipped, and the church pennant—a blue cross on an elongated white triangle—is raised ABOVE the Stars and Stripes, the only pennant or flag permitted to fly above our National flag.

Chapels are provided in all permanent and semiperma-
nent camps and installations of the Army and on most of
the larger shore-based Naval activities. They are equipped
with an altar, a pulpit and lectern, a Communion rail, an
organ, copies of the Hymnal, Army and Navy, and ecclesiastical ornaments for each of the three major faiths. Each
chapel also contains an office and conference rooms for the
chaplains.

No chapel is given a denominational name and no chapel
is permanently assigned for the use of a particular religious
group. It is the rule that the religious symbols of one faith
are removed after the service of that faith is over. Every
effort is made to have each chapel an all faith chapel, a sym-
bol of the religious faith and aspiration of all men of good
will.

As units move up toward the front beyond the areas
where chapels are provided, the ingenuity of the chaplain is
challenged to build or improvise a building for divine worship. The November 1944 and January 1945 issues of *The
Chaplain* contain instances of Army, Marine, Seabee, and
Navy chaplains' efforts in providing chapels for personnel.
They are indications not only of the chaplains' efforts but
of the interest of the men in working to provide for themselves an adequate place of worship.

Nowhere is the downright resourcefulness of overseas
chaplains better illustrated than in the hundreds of unique
chapels they have designed and built. Constructed often out
of makeshift materials and thrown up by the sweat and
brawn of volunteer and spare time labor of worship-loving

servicemen, they are found from the Aleutians to the South
Pacific.

Many of these overseas chapels are memorials. One was
built in a Bougainville jungle in honor of a 19-year-old
Texas soldier, first of the infantry battalion to lose his life
on the island. In the British Solomon Island Protectorate
stands a chapel which was built by 4000 natives. Of thatch,
and with a native-carved mother-of-pearl inlaid altar, it
has been presented to the American people in honor of the
1600 war dead who gave their lives on Guadalcanal.

An AAF Thunderbolt fighter group stationed at an advance airfield in Italy had the first stone-block chapel in
the Mediterranean Theater. When a large tent was no
longer available, Chaplain ———— and his assistant drafted
blueprints and toured the surrounding country for necessary supplies. Actual construction by skilled Italian labor
and interested soldiers was completed in two weeks. Their
bell is from a monastery, donated by present owners of the
building who were impressed by the American soldiers'
persistent efforts to provide themselves with a place of worship. The cost of the structure is being met with volunteer
contributions from the pilots, ground officers and enlisted
men of the group.

At a North African air service command depot, the
chaplain held chapel for more than a year in hangars, mess
halls, tents and open air—how and where he could. Then
the chaplain and his GI volunteers got together on a chapel.
Original plans for the chapel, 73 feet long, 24 feet wide,
with a seating capacity of 250, were drawn up by a draftsman sergeant at the depot. Arched windows were designed
and constructed by another sergeant and a corporal. Car-
penters and construction men carried on both their work
and supervision of the civilians. Aircraft electricians in-
stalled wiring and fixtures. A private designed the altar, pul-

pit, and reading table, and two non-coms, a draftsman, and a carpenter–sheet-metal worker constructed a steeple and bell tower. Every board in it was salvaged from airplane packing boxes. The men call it "Everyman's Chapel."

In New Guinea stands one of the most beautiful chapels in the area. The sanctuary, office and library, built on a raised wooden platform, occupy 28 feet of the structure's 96 by 30 feet. The rest is taken up with the nave and entrance, floored with coral and covered with sawdust. Wooden benches set on cocoanut logs will seat 375 persons. The balsam pole, tarpaper and thatch roof slants high and there is a steeple in the front. The lower front of the chapel and the very top of the tower, the belfry itself, are covered with pungle (the stem of the sago palm) and the upper front of the building and the lower part of the tower are covered with a basket weave of sago-palm leaves. Inside the chapel are plywood panels framed with cocoanut poles, a panel altar and communion rail. The tabernacle, stained with a brown native dye like the other furnishings, is octagon-shaped, with a slanted roof. Behind the altar and across the whole back of the sanctuary is a wall of upright bamboo poles, and the centerpiece over the tabernacle is a raised rounded cross of smaller bamboo poles. Army nurses made the altar cloth of parachute cloth and lined the tabernacle with the same silken material.

Somewhere on a South Pacific Island, chapel chimes come from four large 4-caliber anti-aircraft shells. An ingenious hand-crank affair permits clappers to strike in the empty shells which were cut different lengths for variety of tone.

As one approaches the actual fighting zone these improvised chapels give place to even more primitive arrangements. A service may be held in the space around the jeep on which the chaplain has spread his portable equipment. An altar may be a plank supported by ammunition boxes with the soldiers sitting on their helmets in the mud. Or the chaplain may have a small canvas tent arranged in a jungle clearing with the men kneeling before it. If it is very close to the battleline, the open-air church is apt to be flanked by fox holes and the service may be interrupted by periodic dives for safety as an enemy plane flies over or an occasional shell comes in.

Certain special situations bring their own problems and opportunities. For example, when an assault unit has completed its training, it is shipped to a staging area in preparation for overseas movement. For reasons of security the men are cut off from all means of communication with their homes. The regular routine of training is replaced by the intensive preparations of men and equipment for movement into the theater of operations. Obviously the chaplain in such a situation has an unusual opportunity. Many men realize for the first time the seriousness of the adventure upon which they are embarked. The chaplain will make every effort to prepare men spiritually for the dangers which lie before them. It is customary to make it possible for every serviceman who desires to do so to receive Holy Communion. Not infrequently men will seek baptism or make a first profession of religious faith.

The chaplain on the transport is responsible not only for the religious services aboard ship but also for the program of recreation and education. The crowded conditions of a transport and the voyage across the vast reaches of the Pacific create a challenging opportunity for the chaplain. Daily services are held on most transports and in almost every case they are attended by large numbers of men. The sports, the amateur dramatics, the music, the motion pictures, the ship's library, the lectures on the new lands toward which the men are sailing, are all part of the transport chaplain's task and all help immeasurably to keep up morale and good spirits during the monotony of the voyage.

If by any chance a chaplain is captured and is detained by the enemy, the Geneva Convention provides that he shall be given a full opportunity to minister to his fellow prisoners. Forty-three chaplains at present are detained by Germany and Japan.

v

Important as are the services of worship, many chaplains feel that their most significant work is the pastoral ministry to individual men and women. The chaplain stands in a unique relationship to the enlisted personnel of the Armed Forces. He is the only commissioned officer whom the soldier or sailor can approach directly without seeking the permission of his first sergeant or a division officer. The chaplain does not exercise command. He, therefore, is not responsible for the administration of discipline, and the soldier or sailor with a "gripe" or a personal problem will talk far more freely with the chaplain than with any other officer.

Men come to chaplains with every conceivable kind of problem. It may be that there is a special reason why a soldier or sailor wants a pass or a furlough. His request has been refused and he comes to the chaplain to enlist his aid. It may be that there is trouble at home—financial trouble, or illness, or a difficulty in personal relationships between the man and his wife. The large number of war marriages on short acquaintance and without the possibility of a normal home life increases tremendously the problems of adjustment in this field. It may be that he is unhappy in the Army or Navy. He cannot get along with the men with whom he is thrown in constant contact in the close quarters of ship or barracks. Or he cannot get along with his noncommissioned officer or officers. He has a particular skill which the service ignores, while it requires him to perform less specialized work of a highly distasteful nature.

The problem may be one that is distinctly moral and religious—the fear of death; scruples about the whole sorry business of engaging in war; remorse for a wrong that has been done; a loss of faith, due to any one of a score of causes; or a groping for faith on the part of a man whose background is for all practical purposes pagan.

Whatever the problem may be, the chaplain will listen sympathetically and with understanding. Frequently he will refer the soldier or sailor to an agency better equipped to deal with the situation than the chaplain himself. Occasionally he will be able to present the case for consideration by the proper military authorities. Always, he will try to be a true counselor and friend. Always, he will remember that he is not primarily a social worker or a psychiatrist but a minister of religion and that his particular function is to bring to bear the resources and the techniques of religion. During the month of September 1944, Army chaplains alone reported 8,400,000 pastoral contacts, a striking illustration of the fact that men in difficulty turn to their chaplain for help.

A special aspect of the chaplain's pastoral work is his ministry to the sick and wounded in the hospital. Regulations provide that whenever a patient appears to be in imminent danger of death, a chaplain shall be notified and that chaplains shall be faithful in their ministrations, not only to the dying but to all who are in the hospital. It would be impossible to estimate the number of suffering, anxious, and discouraged men to whom chaplains have brought the consolation and the courage of religious faith.

Frightened boys in the hospital for the first time in their lives, facing a major operation, are emotionally and spiritually prepared for the operating room by the chaplain. He is able to assure them that the Army and Navy have at their disposal the finest medical skill and the finest equipment the country affords, and he is able by the Sacraments and by a simple prayer to remind the lad of the overruling Providence of God. Dying boys again and again have died in peace because of the ministrations of a chaplain. Lonely, despondent boys, through the long weeks and months of convalescence, are helped by the chaplain to endure the monotony and to face bravely and without bitterness the life that awaits them after their discharge.

Another group with a special need for the chaplain consists of the men in confinement. Most of them are minor offenders confined in brigs or guardhouses. Some who are guilty of more serious offenses are in rehabilitation centers. A few are in federal prisons or penitentiaries. To all the chaplain comes with his message of hope and forgiveness, and the possibility, by God's help, of a new beginning. In ministering to prisoners the chaplain needs all the wisdom and grace which is available. He must never condone offenses. He must avoid the kind of sympathy which leads a prisoner to indulge in self-pity or which creates bitterness and resentment against military authority. On the other hand, he must never become hard or cynical. He must always remember that the great majority of youthful offenders have not been guilty of moral turpitude but of carelessness and misdemeanors. The chaplain must exhibit a rare combination of firmness and of friendship. When he does he will be able to lead men who have made a mistake into a better understanding of their duty to themselves and their God.

The chaplain is also charged with a special responsibility to recruits. Every group of recruits coming into an Army or Navy Reception Center is addressed by a chaplain. He explains to them the religious program of the Armed Forces. He tells them that he is available for personal conferences. He speaks to them of the moral and religious implications of discipline and of the problems they will face, as many of them are away from home for the first time. He encourages them to write home regularly because he knows that there are no more powerful influences for good in a man's life than frequent contact with the loved ones he has left behind. In a word, the chaplain does everything he can to help the recruit make a rapid and normal adjustment to the new situation in which he finds himself.

The chaplain in the Army Reception Center is specifically charged with the duty of addressing recruits on the subject of sex hygiene. A line officer and a medical officer deal with the disciplinary and physical aspects of the problem. The chaplain speaks from the point of view of morals and religion. He will appeal to the men's innate sense of decency and fair play. He will emphasize the ideal of our bodies as temples of God. He will give sound counsel on the avoidance of temptation and he will indicate the religious resources available in Sacraments and prayer.

While it is true that the chaplain's primary task is that of a minister of religion, there is one other field in which he has a direct interest. Regulations provide that the chaplain will be the consultant of commanding officers not only in matters of religion and morals, but also in morale. An Army Manual says:

It is the chaplain's function to stimulate or inspire men through the medium of religion to an idealism which finds its fruition in loyalty, courage and contentment, the very essence of good morale. . . . He should neglect no opportunity to help both officers and men to maintain a cheerful and courageous spirit, with unshaken faith in the high cause which they serve, through both the monotony of noncombat service and the trying ordeals of combat service.

"The monotony of noncombat service"—the phrase calls up pictures of little groups of men serving in lonely outposts, thousands of miles from home, without the recreational facilities that are available in larger installations and with none of the psychological compensations that come with combat service. There are hundreds of chaplains serving in situations like this, doing their utmost by precept and example to build up the morale of officers and men. Chaplains in these isolated posts very often go far beyond their regularly assigned duties, as they arrange recreational activities and a varied educational program for the men's off-duty hours.

VI

The chaplain in the Army or Navy inescapably is brought face to face with the reality of the religious differences which exist among us. A Roman Catholic chaplain cannot administer Holy Communion to a Protestant soldier. A Protestant chaplain cannot hear the confession of a Roman Catholic and grant him Absolution nor can he say Mass. A Jewish chaplain cannot perform the sacramental rites of the Christian church. Neither a Protestant nor a Catholic chaplain can minister fully to a Jewish serviceman. How do the Army and Navy deal with the problem?

First, they recognize the principle of religious liberty upon which America is built. This means that no chaplain shall be asked to perform any act which is contrary to the faith and practice of his church. A minister, priest, or rabbi coming into the chaplaincy does not lose his identity as an official representative of his own faith. The services which he conducts will be the services that are normal and customary to him and to the religious body he represents. The Army or Navy does not tell him how to worship or what to preach.

Second, the same principle of religious liberty means that every man and woman in the Armed Forces has the right to the full exercise of his or her religion. A Roman Catholic has the right to attend Mass on every Sunday and Holy Day of Obligation. A Protestant has the right to the ministrations of a Protestant minister and to receive Holy Communion. Members of Protestant denominations that require their members to receive Communion only at the hands of their own clergy have a right to have their faith and practice respected. Jewish men and women have the right to attend the services of their faith, including especially the observance of the High Holy Days. Occasionally, of course, military necessity will prevent attendance upon a particular service.

Finally, the principle of religious liberty, while it in no way limits a chaplain in the direct, positive teaching of the truth as he sees it, does definitely rule out any attempt at proselytizing and any attack upon the faith of another.

How are these principles applied in practice? In the Army there are three chaplains assigned to an infantry regiment. In most cases, one will be Catholic and two, Protestant. In the divisional artillery there are two chaplains. Usually one will be Catholic and one, Protestant. On a large post or station there may be as many as fifteen or twenty chaplains. In that case there will normally be one Jewish chaplain and the others will be divided between the Catholic and Protestant faiths. Thus, in a great majority of cases, there will be present with troops both Catholic and Protestant chaplains, and in large installations there will also be a Jewish chaplain.

The question arises, what happens in small posts, in separate battalions, on isolated islands in the Aleutians or the South Pacific, in the Greenland Base or the Persian Gulf Command, or on an isolated airfield in Burma or China? Obviously there are hundreds of places where there will be a small detachment with a single chaplain. How does he meet the problem?

In such a situation, each chaplain will remember that he is appointed to be "the friend, counselor and guide, without discrimination, to all members of the command to which he is assigned, regardless of race, creed or sect." This statement from Army Regulations points out that there are many services which a devoted chaplain can render to men of other faiths than his own. Then, he will make every effort to bring in other clergy to meet the distinctly religious needs of men to whom he is not competent to minister. The isolated Protestant chaplain will endeavor to bring in a Catholic priest, either another chaplain or a civilian, to say Mass for his Catholic men. An isolated Catholic chaplain will endeavor to bring in a Protestant minister to provide Holy Communion for his Protestant men. Christian chaplains, in the absence of a Jewish chaplain or civilian rabbi, can assist the Jewish man of the command to form a congregation, and to conduct services for themselves. The isolated chaplain may obtain literature from the appropriate denominational publishing houses and carry on a literary ministry. As a last resort, he may conduct a general service of such a nature as to help all men to a deeper faith in the God who is the common Father of us all.

Finally, when a man is dying and no chaplain of his particular faith is present, any chaplain of any denomination can read the appropriate prayers of the man's own faith. More than once a Protestant or Jewish chaplain has held a crucifix before the eyes of a dying Catholic, and a Catholic chaplain has offered a prayer for a dying Protestant or Jew.

VII

The ultimate goal of all military training is the moment when our ships or our troops engage the enemy. All the months of training, all the lavish provision of equipment, all the sacrifice involved in separation from one's family and the interruption of one's civilian career, find their reason for existence in the day of battle. How the chaplain himself behaves in battle and how the men to whom he has ministered behave is the final test.

Consider any one of the hundreds of Navy chaplains assigned to ships of the fleet. They know the long monotony and the vast distances of the Pacific, the restricted life of the ship, the trying days of storm. When the alert sounds and the ship is cleared for action, the chaplain is inescapably involved in all the peril of combat. Every bomb, every torpedo, every shell is aimed at him just as surely as at the other members of the crew. Amid the flame and shock of battle, in the sick bay with the wounded, or going over the side at the order, "Abandon ship!" the chaplain fully shares the dangers with his men and brings to them the comfort and strength of religious faith. Chaplains with the Seabees, the Marine Corps, and the Coast Guard also share the common dangers, for in all amphibious operations of the Naval Services, chaplains have gone into the thick of battle with their units.

Consider any one of the hundreds of chaplains assigned to the Army Air Forces. Normally, he does not fly on a combat mission. But he does see the planes off, often after a brief prayer with the officers and men who are about to fly over enemy-held territory. Then, with the remainder of the ground crew and headquarters, he "sweats it out," waiting for the planes to come back. The time finally arrives when they are due, and one by one they come in. Some are riddled with flak. Some are carrying wounded and dead. Some do not come back at all. The chaplain meets the incoming planes. He ministers to the wounded. He writes letters of condolence to the families of the dead. And then, at the evening mess, he sits down at a table where there are vacant places. There will be young officers there who, a few hours before, saw their friends go down in flaming planes. Yet the life of the squadron must go on and the war must go on, and the chaplain must do what he can to bring the stability and the courage and the faith which makes men able to bear the strain, day after day, month after month, for twenty, thirty, forty, or fifty missions.

Or consider the chaplain with the Army Ground Forces when they move into the lines. There is, first of all, the endless marching through the steaming heat of the jungle or through the rain, the cold, and mud of the Western Front; the unbelievable weariness and discomfort; the long, sleepless nights in fox holes; the bombing and strafing by planes; the crash of incoming shells. The chaplain is there with his unit, not usually in the very front line, to be sure, but at the battalion first aid station or the regimental collecting station. There he ministers to the wounded and dying, bringing to them the strength and assurance of religious faith. Occasionally he administers first aid. Often he takes down a message from a wounded man to be sent to his loved ones back home. Frequently he goes to the forward positions to minister to a dying man. At times he remains in an aid station with the wounded who cannot be moved, in the face of an enemy counter-attack destined to overrun the position. When the action dies down, he will make his way from one machine gun post to another, dropping into the trench, giving to each man a word of greeting, administering the Sacraments, and saying for them all a prayer for God's protection and for the strength to do their duty.

Always after action there is the sad duty of the burial of the dead. Perhaps there will be a Graves Registration Service Officer present, in which case the chaplain simply reads the service at the graveside. Frequently the chaplain will himself act as the Graves Registration Officer, in charge of the search of the battlefield, the identification of the bodies, the collection and safeguarding of the personal effects, the burial, and the marking and proper registration of the graves. When death occurs aboard ships of the fleet, Navy chaplains perform solemn rites for burial at sea. Frequently they are called upon to conduct memorial services in tribute to the memory of their departed comrades.

Statistics are cold things when they refer to the tragedy and the heroism of war, but the figures speak more effectively than thousands of words concerning the valor of chaplains who "did not love their lives even in face of death." The latest figures released by the Office of the Chief of Chaplains of the Army list the following casualties up to the 31st of December 1944:

Killed in Action	40
Died in the Service	47
Wounded	105
Detained by the Enemy	38
Died while Detained by the Enemy	1
Missing in Action	1

The Navy Department reports the following casualties among its chaplains:

Killed in Action	4
Killed in Operational Accidents	3
Died in the Service	5
Wounded	22
Detained by the Enemy	5
Missing	1

Three hundred eighty-four Army chaplains have received a total of four hundred fifty-nine decorations:

Distinguished Service Cross	15
Legion of Merit	35
Silver Star	74
Oak Leaf Cluster, Silver Star	2
Soldier's Medal	8
Bronze Star	165
Oak Leaf Cluster, Bronze Star	4
Air Medal	1
Purple Heart	145
Oak Leaf Cluster, Purple Heart	6
Croix de Guerre	3
Sultan of Morocco	1

Navy chaplains have received a total of forty-nine decorations in World War II:

Legion of Merit	6
Silver Star	6
Bronze Star	4
Navy and Marine Corps Medal	3
Purple Heart	22
Individual Commendations	8

It seems clear that the devotion of the chaplains in the Army and Navy is not only bringing the ministry of religion to millions of men and women in the Armed Forces today, but that it is laying the foundation for the work of all the churches in the post-war world. The fact that the church cared enough to send priests and ministers and rabbis from the security of their civilian posts into the loneliness and hazards of battle will not be lost upon returning soldiers and sailors. They will recall that the chaplains were not compelled to enter the service. They came freely because of their desire to serve, and that service will not be altogether forgotten.

NOTE. This chapter has been passed and approved by the Public Relations authorities of the Army and Navy.

· 5 ·

A Soldier's Second Thoughts

THE subject of the following chapter has been entitled "a soldier's second thoughts"—a title to which I bring attention, because it calls for both an apology and an explanation. In the next few pages I shall endeavor to give some sort of sketch of the relation of the war to the spiritual life of servicemen, and of some of the more evident problems, moral and religious, which war has raised in the minds of the millions of men who are serving overseas. The words "second thoughts" have been here used advisedly, for after all a fighting man's first thoughts must be devoted to the immediate job, the performance of whatever mission in the field lies before him. Then, too, there is a danger in "second thoughts," a danger that in such thoughts we lose the living immediacy of actual life and find ourselves playing instead the part of the spider, spinning a web out of ourselves. Especially is this true of writing on the role of religion in life, for religion is something whose essence must be felt rather than logically explained or understood in the narrower sense of the word. In its union of imagination and feeling it seeks its natural expression rather through the poetic means of metaphor and paradox, and, in its uncontrollable habit of being all things to all men, it leaps over the conventional boundaries of language and eludes that sort of sober definition upon which all discussion should be based.

The first difficulty that arises on discussing a problem so vast and abstruse as religion is its very uncommunicability. A man's private belief is usually the last thing you learn about him, especially in the service, where questions and knowledge of immediate practical importance must perforce come first. There is generally no subject on which a serviceman is so inarticulate as the tenets of his belief. This is especially true of those who are professing Protestants, whose connection with any church has been only occasional, and who have not had the advantage of the long indoctrination and practice required of all Catholics.

In addition to this problem of the inarticulateness of the average man's faith, there is, of course, the limitation of any one man's experience. My own personal experience under the tension of battle has been limited to less than a week, and of the long days of nervous anticipation, exhaustion, mental and physical fatigue, and hunger, I can speak only secondhand. I enter these autobiographical remarks only in extenuation for any remarks which follow. Of course, it is impossible for one man to speak for so many millions; the best he can do is to be as honest as he can to his own limited range of experience.

There is a good deal of false optimism about the growth of religious faith among servicemen which hovers especially about circles not immediately associated with the war. I speak of the notion made famous by the remark that "there are no atheists in fox holes." This to my mind is a gross misconception which is denied by all actual facts; it is not only untrue, but dangerous in its implication that faith is an easy thing, quickly acquired in the stress of circumstances. The verdict of experience is far otherwise, for not only are there many men who are resolutely opposed to any sort of faith, in whatever guise it may express itself, but the too easy identification of a fox hole variety with the principles of a real and creative faith is a dangerous obstruction to any true understanding of the requirements and self-discipline which lie at the very base of religion.

Any experience, whether brief or prolonged, with any number of servicemen soon reveals that religious ideas of every shade, from belief in its highest form to an active and vociferous atheism, exist side by side. We have always known this, and the attempt to atone for the horrible irrationality of war by insisting that it breeds religious faith is nothing short of intellectual dishonesty.

In order to know how to deal with a problem so complex as that of religious faith, we must first come to terms with the facts. I can speak only from the limitations of my own experience, but if the men with whom I served are any sort of cross section of the people of the nation, the truth of the matter is that for nearly half of them the so-called "religious problem" did not exist, either in respect to outward observance, or inward speculative and moral dilemmas. Life was accepted, enjoyed whenever possible, fought about, laughed over, lived to the hilt, in fact almost anything but thought about in any abstract, final way. Those who have had the good fortune to read the books of Ernie Pyle will have seen there the average American's enormous love of life: his humor, homesickness, ingenuity, bravery in the face of danger; his boredom, hatred and disgust with war. But none of these qualities is a specifically religious one. It is their earthliness, their very closeness to the vivid, impulsive life of the senses that makes them so refreshing, so naïve, so unspeculative.

The common attitude of men in battle is that life or death is a matter of luck and a man praying in a fox hole is usually praying that the next bullet won't have his name on it, not that it won't have someone else's in the fox hole next to him. Prayer of this sort is a form of mental relief: an appeal for self-preservation—not from hell but from death. Much of the apparent growth of religion today among servicemen overseas is due to this fear of death. There is a well-substantiated story that some of the marines getting ready to make landings on the island of Bougainville in the Solomons prepared themselves by hanging both a cross and the tablets of the law about their necks. Here is Pascal's wager with a vengeance! Viewed in such a manner, religion becomes a sort of last-minute everlasting life insurance which can be bought with low premiums and pays big dividends. I repeat this story not to fill the already well-stocked larders of cynicism about the religious question, but as an indication of the real seriousness of the problem. For a real, enduring faith is not bought so cheaply and we must guard against a rise in religious temperature which is due solely to the heat of the surroundings. A religion based on the self-preservative instincts of its followers, instead of that inward moral growth which comes with a desire for service and self-discipline, will collapse as soon as its need has been fulfilled. It will certainly play little part in the confused and trying period after the war when the truly religious qualities of unselfishness, patience, and understanding will be needed more than ever.

The immediate effects of war and the environment of the service tend, I believe, to weaken most men's expression and practice of religious faith, except in those moments of great crisis when each individual stands alone. The routine of barracks life, the nature of military training and of battle itself, emphasize the active, decisive, communal sides of man's nature. This experience has been a profoundly healthy one for a great many people, tending to bring them out of themselves, forcing them to make decisions, to join in and share the lives of their fellows, and perhaps converting many religious natures of an introspective type to a more objective point of view. However, the boredom and staleness which creep into so much of service life, the limited objectives of war, the mixed motives of battle—for war to the individual soldier is a blunt question of survival, not

the distant realization of an international ideal—all these
and many of the other problems which war thrusts into the
lives of soldiers have done much to crust over men's minds
and hearts—now long familiar with the suddenness and
finality of death—and numb the pain once felt for the loss
of those who have shared so much, leaving behind nothing
but the fierce necessity to feel.

But the greatest loss of religion is among the young men.
Still emotionally immature and inexperienced, they suddenly find themselves thrown into crowded quarters and
forced to get along with all sorts of men at the same time
that the former security of their home life is lost. No longer
responsible to anyone but themselves, they find it an easy
matter to pick up the light-hearted and casual cynicism of
their more experienced bunkmates and to let religious matters drift gradually out of sight.

The first step in the building of a real religious faith must
lie in the feeling of the necessity to believe. But intense feeling is a Janus-faced quality and defiance lies next to faith.
The greatest problem, however, which religion faces is not
the attitude of defiance which comes from disillusionment,
but the inertia and too-easy acceptance of belief dissociated
from its living sources. For religion is an active attitude
adopted towards life, based on a faith which finds its understanding in action. Such a faith leads a man forward
through life instead of being merely an appeal in moments
of helplessness.

I have seen many forms of belief and disbelief in every
group of men. There were some men who seemed to draw

their energy and courage from a defiance which denied all but the grim facts of war, as if, after such things, a religious belief were a betrayal of their allegiance to the depth and bitterness of their experience. Once or twice in one's experience in the service one meets a man who has a quiet sincerity and simplicity of faith to which no words can do justice. Such men are rare—I myself have known only one —but such a faith, in its cheerfulness under all conditions and its breadth of understanding and humility, once recognized, can never be forgotten.

But such well-defined emotional attitudes towards the problem of war as it affects religious belief are not common, for such attitudes can only arise with a consciousness of the problem. The majority of men, in so far as I have been able to observe, live on two levels of experience which often have little connection. The foremost is the commonplace acceptance of things as they exist, which does not probe beneath the surface for any ultimate explanation of the meaning of suffering or of evil. The other level of experience appears in those brief moments of emotional crisis when, for lack of any earthly help, men resort to prayer.

There is a widespread notion that a prayerful attitude accompanies a man like a guardian angel throughout the various phases of combat and does not desert him once the crisis is over. From my own observation, the facts are not so. Battle is a preëminently practical affair, and all of a man's physical and mental resources are concentrated on the one most immediate, most natural and tangible mode of salvation available to him—action. For it is action, immediate and decisive, which is a man's chief resort and rescue from the paralyzing fear of death, and during the tense emotional excitement of actual combat a man's conscious mind is forever trying to catch up with his unconscious reactions. For fear which men experience in battle is not the metaphysical fear of unspeakable things, Melville's heartless voids and invisible spheres formed in fright: it is the animal fear, direct and physical, which comes over all creatures when they know they are in danger. It is during the moments of waiting and inaction, under artillery fire or bombardment, that most men fall back on prayer, a state of mind which in many cases seems to fade away when the feeling of helplessness is over.

But life in the service, despite the boredom, mud, and tragedy, has given something to those who have shared it which perhaps no other human experience could have supplied. The sense of sharing, of working together for a common goal, whether it be the next objective, hill or river bank, or the more distant and confused ideals of world order, peace, understanding among men: this is something which I believe once experienced will never be lost. For out of such suffering and sacrifice have come to many a closeness and understanding which cuts across all the artificial barriers of race, class, and diversity of background, and there is a new-won realization of the vigor and largeness of the principles of a true democracy.

The greatest difficulty is to know where to find words which can adequately express the strength and capacity for sacrifice of men in battle—words honest, simple, and direct enough to speak the truth. The tradition of Armistice Day and Memorial Day sentiment, of men marching breast forward and falling with their faces to the foe, brought its reaction in many of the poets of the last war who attacked in bitter, trenchant lines "the old lie of 'dulce et decorum est.'" Part of this great rift in feeling is due, as a moment's reflection will show, to the failure to distinguish between what we may call the spirit of battle, with its enlistment of all of a man's energies in a cause greater than self, its quickening of the pulses, concentration of mind, body, and will towards one objective—all the qualities in short which make their appeal to man's desire to live intensely—and on the other hand, the sordidness of the actual reality of war as it is played out in all the cruelty of modern ingenuity.

The fault with both these views is that they are one-sided and fail to express the immediate, living intensity of feeling, the "horror, glory, and boredom" at the base of actual experience; and just as war is no Stoic's paradise of noble gestures, just as surely there are moments which strike beneath the grim external reality of war with its madness and confusion, and bring their reward not in happiness but in that profound feeling of comradeship which common sacrifices endured for a common goal alone can give. For in the actual doing of a courageous act, whether it be the rescue of a fellow man or something involving the security of an entire battalion, we become momentarily identified with the act itself; we as individuals cease to live, and we become the intense unity of the act, the desire, the determination. Saint-Exupéry, in that magnificent and profound description of his flight over Arras, describes vividly this feeling. Perhaps if Hobbes had stayed in England during the Puritan Revolution, instead of escaping to France, he would have gathered some material which would have forced him to revise some of his cynical observations on the psychology of human behavior. For such an act of courage is an act of faith: a faith which lies deeper than any abstract principles, and springs from that closeness of man to man which is the living heart of both democracy and religion itself.

A man can fight without a conscious religious belief and do courageous acts, but the man who has lost his faith in his fellow men has cut himself off from the greatest source of meaning which life can offer. For in the end most men do not fight for abstract principles, still less do many fight today for the shadowy tenets of most of our present-day beliefs, but there are few men so cowardly and unfeeling that they will not risk their lives for their own friends. The majority of us live in the fullness of actual facts and events, our passions are attached to the immediate concrete satisfactions of life: the pleasures of family, friends, and interests; and it is for such things that we make sacrifices.

It is this mixture of courage and unpretentiousness of the average man's faith in his fellow men that makes it so difficult to describe. Courage, like all qualities, is an emotionally complex condition in the majority of circumstances, compounded of fear, training, anger, bitterness, and above all, perhaps, the desire not to let one's buddies down. But such as it is, it is the most vivid expression which a man can give of his affirmation of that basic truth of Christianity that only he who loses his life shall save it. However, such sacrifice cannot of course be unhesitatingly attributed to religious belief. Many of the most courageous men I have ever known have been either nonreligious or actually antireligious in nature, and this does not include men whose action in battle can be more fitly attributed to bold recklessness than to the finer moral attributes of courage.

When we begin to explore the broader aspects and implications of war upon the religious life of servicemen, we begin to poach upon the grounds of sociologists and psychologists. The effect of modern warfare upon the structure of society, the long, discouraging years of social readjustment which inevitably follow in the wake of such periods, have been exhaustively discussed from various points of view. We can only guess from the indications we see at present what the long-distance effects of war will be upon the moral and religious life of those who participated. Of these, there are two tendencies of a broadly ethical nature which will perhaps most profoundly affect the attitude of men in the years following the war. The first of these is the regimentation and suppression of individuality which life in the service necessarily involves: factors which are diametrically opposed to the characteristically independent and individualistic temper of American thought. The long hours of wearisome routine, the whole monotony of barracks life in general, tend to suffocate the type of vigorous, independent inquiry and expression upon which the freedom of thought and religious feeling so largely depend. Of course it is easy to overemphasize this effect of military life upon personality, and the source of religion is, after all, independent of the accidents of place and time. Great religious geniuses are not made in the coffee shops of London and the Left Bank of the Seine.

On the other hand, war, by emphasizing the cheapness of life, tends to speed up its tempo and accentuate its impulsive, pleasure-loving side as compensation for the drab routine and strict military discipline of everyday life in the service and, above all, for the consciousness of the imminence of death.

The effect of these tendencies is naturally opposed to the growth of a religious tradition for "war is a savage teacher," as the greatest historian of the ancient world has written, "which brings men's characters down to the level of their fortunes," and the strict external discipline of the armed forces is no substitute for that fine self-discipline which is the root of true religious faith.

But in the end, the final effect of war can be said neither to help nor to hinder the growth of real religious feeling. There is, of course, more apparent irreligion among those people who seize the opportunity to reflect, in the aimlessness of their own inner lives, the external confusion and chaos which they see about them; but also perhaps there is the slow and steady growth of a real religion in some of those who have been brought face to face by personal tragedy with the compulsion and the necessity to believe. Such a faith once won is never lost, for the power which it confers upon the lives of those who have experienced it is an explanation and justification too deep for any words to disperse.

II

These considerations of the effect of war upon the lives of servicemen bring us inevitably back to the basic problem of the role of religion in American life. It would be presumptuous to attempt any sort of synoptic survey of this enormous field within the limits of this short chapter, even if the subject did not lie well outside the competence of the writer. Nevertheless, a few remarks, however brief and inadequate, on some of the aspects of American life and their effect upon the religious currents of our times do seem appropriate here in order to make clear other problems on the relation of religion to the narrower issues of the war.

There is a real danger today, I believe, of religion losing its hold as an effective instrument in the majority of men's lives. Just pick up any newspaper and read the speeches of our national leaders and compare them with those of Jefferson and Lincoln and you cannot help noticing the difference. The same words are there, but there is an unmistakable change in feeling: the difference which comes with an increasing secularization of thought where religion as a vital force has been diluted to the role of a vague emotional stimulant used to hallow the narrower designs of politics.

The greatest danger to active faith in America today, it seems to me, is this persistent tendency of many people, especially among the leaders of philosophical and educational thought, to identify religion with various historic processes and ideas, such as democracy and liberty and that group of ideas which stem from the principles formulated and set forth under the title of the Rights of Man.

The general trend of all such ideas, divorced from their religious foundations, is to deprive man of the ultimate dignity conferred upon him as the ambassador of God. In the democratic emphasis upon men as individuals we are in danger of losing sight of Man in his relation to God, as Saint-Exupéry has so profoundly remarked. For it is with Man, understood in his relation to God, that the only true and meaningful conception of liberty and equality can exist. Understanding this, we may get some glimpse into the full meaning of Christ's teaching, and of the infinite individual demands which it makes.

For the real greatness of religion lies in the very individuality of its challenge and demands. Unlike so much of modern thought, it shifts the center of emphasis from impersonal and social to personal and individual responsibility. In our tendency to lay our troubles at the doors of society, economics, and our Unconscious, we lose sight of the individual and moral foundations of life, of the concrete, practical importance of faith in bringing the world of our ideals closer to the world of facts.

The optimism of the religious view is no easy optimism based on the joys of an illimitable imagination and modest wants, but, springing from a profound understanding of the individual and personal nature of evil, it supplies the kind of hard-won optimism which is grounded upon work and self-sacrifice and a trust in God. Anyone who has read the essays of William James must have felt the challenge and opportunity of his dynamic view of faith as an acceptance of the great wager and an incentive to action which "smelleth the battle afar off."

The great importance of religious faith, especially in times when the individual is in danger of being submerged by the huge impersonal forces of a world at war, lies in its assertion of the importance and freedom of individual effort, and in the restoration of self-confidence in its call to what James has aptly named the "strenuous life."

Now, finally, we come to perhaps the most urgent problem of all in the consideration of the role of religion in the post-war world. What qualifications must it have in order to maintain its position as a vital force in men's lives—a force which will be an incentive to that strenuous life James speaks of: a strength, and enlarger of life's possibilities? Mr. C. E. M. Joad, the eminent British philosopher, has rather taken Christ to task in a recent book for not being more explicit on many of the speculative and so-called practical problems of life—filling in other words the role of philosopher-critic-humorist which Mr. Joad seems to play so admirably for his own country. This, it seems to me, is one of the fundamental errors of insight into the religious question which is made by so many of our intellectual leaders today: people who regard the role of religion as a sort of radio commentator on life's manifold interests rather than as an ultimate judge.

That movement of European thought known as Christian Humanism, which linked the greatest minds from the sixteenth to the eighteenth centuries, is a noble monument in man's spiritual pilgrimage, but in the form in which it flourishes today, it has become such a humanized version of "Christianity not Mysterious" that it well deserves the scornful title, once applied to it by one of our contemporary preachers, of a "How to Win Friends and Influence People Religion."

I believe that the only form of religion which will be able permanently to satisfy the minds and spirits of men who have seen this present struggle in all of its sordidness, confusion, and horror is one which can find real answers through new and spiritually creative paths to the vital problems of life, and it will succeed only in so far as it goes beyond the synthesized versions of culture and progress which have seized so many of the pulpits of our nation.

War has brought millions of men face to face with personal tragedy too deep for any words to utter. It has brought to many men the realization that there is something brute and irrational in the world to which we have given the name of evil, in the face of which only faith, a faith born of suffering, discipline, and prayer, can ever hope to find any sort of ultimate acceptance and peace. But war has also brought its share of bitterness and disillusionment, and many will come from this conflict less religious because the faith which religion demands is a constant struggle with the forces of doubt and disillusionment, and wisdom is not always born of suffering. Anything less than a belief which arises from man's most persistent questions as to the nature of life, and which answers those deep-seated desires to make the world more meaningful, will not be enough.

Religion thus ceases to be metaphysical speculation and becomes a force in the lives of men for, in the final word, religion is not an affair of the head: the heart has its reasons which the head does not know. "We do not believe," Thoreau has remarked, "a tide rises and falls behind every man which can float the British Empire like a chip if he should ever harbor it in his mind."

The question which will be demanded of religion is, "does it make a genuine difference in our lives?" And as in war the success of a strategic or tactical principle is judged by its outcome in the field of battle, so in religion its success or failure will be measured by its ability to illuminate the lives of men with a new and enlarged meaning and purpose.

Just as democracy is not a set of political principles only, but the attitude of mind from which those principles are born, so religion is not to be identified solely with its shifting dogmas and symbols. For many centuries a footprint sufficed to show the disciples of Buddha where Truth had walked. The way of all religion is trodden by the saints, by those who, in the words of St. Paul, have felt that inward force: "not me, but Christ in me."

The problem of religious faith begins and ends in prayer. As in the battlefield the doing of a courageous act is often the gateway to courage, so, in the realm of the spirit, the way to that faith which is courage, action, and the peace that passeth all understanding lies through prayer.

Note: Cleared for publication. Jonathan C. Rice, Captain, U.S.M.C.R.